CAMBRIDGE STUDIES IN
PUBLISHING AND PRINTING HISTORY

The Provincial Book Trade in
Eighteenth-Century England

The Provincial Book Trade in Eighteenth-Century England

JOHN FEATHER

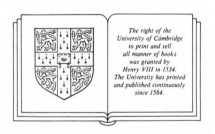

The right of the
University of Cambridge
to print and sell
all manner of books
was granted by
Henry VIII in 1534.
The University has printed
and published continuously
since 1584.

CAMBRIDGE UNIVERSITY PRESS

CAMBRIDGE

LONDON   NEW YORK   NEW ROCHELLE
MELBOURNE   SYDNEY

Published by the Press Syndicate of the University of Cambridge
The Pitt Building, Trumpington Street, Cambridge CB2 1RP
32 East 57th Street, New York, NY 10022, USA
10 Stamford Road, Oakleigh, Melbourne 3166, Australia

First published 1985

Printed in Great Britain at
the University Press, Cambridge

Library of Congress catalogue card number: 84–29308

British Library cataloguing in publication data
Feather, John
The provincial book trade in eighteenth-century
England. – (Cambridge studies in publishing
and printing history)
1. Book industries and trade – England – History
– 18th century
I. Title
338.4′7686′0942   Z325
ISBN 0 521 30334 6

FP

IN MEMORIAM

H.G.P.

MAGISTER HORUM ARTIUM

Contents

Illustrations

Preface

The English provincial book trade has been the subject of serious historical study for rather more than a century. In 1879, W. H. Allnutt, an Assistant at the Bodleian, read a paper on 'Printers and printing in the provincial towns of England and Wales' to the first annual meeting of the Library Association, held at Oxford. Allnutt's pioneering work was an account of the introduction of printing into provincial towns, and over the next eighty years was followed by numerous local studies, most of them by librarians or by those amateur historians who have contributed so much to our knowledge of the minutiae of the history of provincial England. Many of these studies are excellent, soundly based as they are on documents in record offices and private archives, and on the study of provincially printed books to be found in the local collections of our public libraries. Printing, especially book printing, has inevitably attracted the greatest attention; it is more exciting than bookselling, and its products can be seen and handled on library shelves. In 1959, Paul Morgan summarised the achievements of his predecessors in a lecture on 'English provincial printing' delivered in Birmingham. In 1977, appropriately in Oxford and addressing the Rare Books Group of the Library Association, Morgan showed that histories or directories of the trade had been published for eighteen of the thirty-nine English counties; work is now in progress on similar studies of at least nine others.

Despite all this effort, however, surprisingly little is known of the provincial book trade as an economic entity. We have lists of names, trades, places, and dates, but no attempt has previously been made to flesh out these bare bones of knowledge. This book is an attempt to do just that. Without the work of the last century such a synthesis would have been impossible, and it is difficult even now. Yet I do not believe that the attempt is premature. Book history, including the commercial history of books, is an increasingly popular subject. Regional studies of it are proceeding apace, and I hope that I have at least provided a perspective within which such local studies of the trade can be viewed more sharply.

Preface

I have been primarily concerned to solve a single problem: how those living outside London obtained their books. In considering this problem, I have inevitably confronted others: the structure and organisation of the book trade; its growth and development; the demand for books in the provinces; and the economics of provincial bookselling and printing. Nevertheless, I hope that I have not strayed too far from my central theme of book supply, or from my central thesis that the provincial trade, despite all the interest in its printing activities, was essentially distributive.

I make no claim to have said the last word on these matters, and indeed it is my hope that this first attempt at a general history of the provincial trade will stimulate further local research. I do believe, however, that the essence of my argument is accurate, and that local studies will be enhanced by being placed in this national context. We live at the end of the age in which the printed word has been the unchallenged medium of mass communication. Perhaps that is why we are so fascinated by its history and influence, and why its importance in the broader history of our society is becoming more generally recognised. This book is offered as one small contribution to our understanding of the dissemination and significance of printing, and the crucial role which it has played in the history of western culture in the last five hundred years.

JOHN FEATHER

Loughborough University
July 1984

Acknowledgements

My last conversation with the dedicatee of this book was about the provincial book trade. I was engaged on a cataloguing project which was becoming tedious, and I relieved the tedium by indexing the names of booksellers whose names appeared in the documents being catalogued. I was puzzled by the recurrence of certain provincial names in prospectuses and imprints, and asked Graham Pollard if he knew why these names and not others appeared there. We agreed that a more detailed study of the provincial trade was needed; I hope that my readers will think that we were right.

If Graham Pollard inspired me by exhortation, David Foxon has done so by example. His name appears in several notes, but that is merely the tip of the iceberg of my intellectual indebtedness to him. His own work, our conversations over the last decade and, not least, his careful and critical reading of an earlier draft of this book have helped me beyond measure in attaining whatever merit this work might have.

The bulk of the research was done while I was Munby Fellow in Bibliography at Cambridge University Library in 1977–78. I can only hope that the results will repay the confidence of the Electors. The late E. B. Ceadel, J. C. T. Oates, David McKitterick, Brian Jenkins, and their colleagues welcomed me as a friend, and were unfailingly helpful to their demanding guest. John Oates was equally kind in smoothing my way to a Fellowship at Darwin College, where the then Master, Fellows, and students provided a memorably agreeable social context for my stay in Cambridge.

The editors of this series, David McKitterick and Terry Belanger, have both read the typescript with the utmost care, and I owe to both of them many valuable suggestions. Needless to say, I accept sole responsibility for what is written here.

Part of the research was undertaken with an award from the Small Grants Fund of the British Academy, which I gratefully acknowledge.

My former colleague Paul Morgan has freely shared his great knowledge of the provincial trade, as have many others in this field. It

Acknowledgements

is almost invidious to select names, but I should particularly like to mention Bernard Barr, R. J. Chamberlaine-Brothers, Peter Freshwater, Richard Goulden, David Stoker, and Peter Wallis. Another former colleague, Sheila Edward, checked many references and greatly assisted in the proof reading, among many other kindnesses.

I am grateful to the librarians and archivists who made materials available to me, and wish to acknowledge their permission to print documents which are copyright to their owners. I am particularly grateful to Mr John Cheney, of John Cheney and Sons Ltd, Banbury, for allowing me to consult and quote the archives of his firm and family.

A lecture based on some of the material used in this book was delivered to several audiences in the United States in 1981 and 1982. I should like to thank them, and my hosts, for their generous reception, and for the valuable stimulus which an American audience always provides.

Mrs Cynthia Robinson has coped valiantly with my bad typing and worse handwriting.

Lady Eden is reported to have said that there were times when she felt that the Suez Canal was flowing through her drawing room. Sarah Feather has lived with the provincial book trade for as long as I, and has taught me that an author's thanks to his wife are no mere convention.

Note on Sources

This book is based upon the published work of many scholars, especially on that of those antiquaries who have combed public and private repositories for the documentary evidence of the history of the book trade, and those who have compiled directories and bibliographies. My notes bear witness to the magnitude of their contribution. I have not, however, felt it necessary to give a full list of my sources, although I must mention here two basic works without which the study of the English book trade would be impossible. Both are now sadly out of date, and in need of replacement, yet they are still indispensable: H. R. Plomer's *A dictionary of the printers and booksellers who were at work in England, Scotland and Ireland from 1668 to 1725*, published by the Bibliographical Society in 1922; and the continuation by Plomer, G. H. Bushnell, and E. R. McC. Dix, *A dictionary of the printers and booksellers who were at work in England, Scotland and Ireland from 1726–1775*, published by the same society in 1932. I have already published a list of other work on the trade in *The English provincial book trade. A checklist of secondary sources* (Oxford (Oxford Bibliographical Society, occasional publication, 16), 1981).

I have, however, undertaken a good deal of archival research to supplement previously published work, and some notes on this may be useful. In the Public Record Office, I have searched systematically for the wills of members of the trade proved in the Prerogative Court of Canterbury (PROB 11); for cases relating to the trade in the Court of Chancery, especially among the Chancery Master's Exhibits (C 104) and in the records of the Vice-Master and Commissioners in Bankruptcy (B 1–6); and for records of apprenticeship (IR 1/45–53). The records of the Sun, Alliance, and London Insurance Group Ltd, partly still in the possession of the company, and partly in the Guildhall Library, London, proved useful in several respects. In the Bodleian Library, Oxford, I have used the invaluable archives of John Nichols, acquired by the Library in 1975–76 (MS Eng. lett. b. 11–19; c. 354–72), the letter book of Kincaid and Bell (MS Eng. lett. c. 20, 21), and various documents in the Gough and Rawlinson collections. The University Archives at Oxford provided some useful wills and inventories. It gave me particular pleasure to use some of the manuscript material (as well as many printed books) in the Munby Collection at Cambridge University Library. The British Library has provided a few letters and minor documents, and I have also made use of the Minute Book of the proprietors of *The General Evening Post*, formerly in the possession of the late Wilmarth S. Lewis, and now the property of Yale University as part of the Lewis collection at Farmington, Connecticut.

Among local records I have made much use of the one substantial archive of a provincial bookseller known to me, that of John Clay of Daventry in the Northamptonshire Record Office. The Record Offices of Bristol, Essex, Gloucestershire, Humberside, and Staffordshire, have also provided material. Mr John Cheney kindly permitted me to use the archives of his family firm, still in the firm's possession in Banbury.

Finally, I have made use, to a far greater extent than may be superficially apparent, of the books printed in the provinces. This was largely undertaken from the substantial collections of the Bodleian and Cambridge University libraries. In this context, I ought to add that the British Library entries for the Eighteenth-Century Short Title Catalogue became available, through BLAISE, only as this book was in the final stages of preparation for the press. My successors will, of course, take advantage of this valuable new tool of eighteenth-century studies; I have been unable to do so, but I do not believe that my conclusions have been materially affected by the lack.

Note on Dates and Places

All year dates have been normalised to a year beginning on 1 January, except in direct quotations. Dates before 2 September 1753 are Old Style, and after that day New Style.

Place names are given in their usual modern form. Counties, however, are those which existed in the eighteenth century, and do not, in many cases, correspond to the boundaries in force since the Local Government Act of 1972. I have roughly defined 'provincial' as more than twenty miles from London.

Abbreviations

The following abbreviations are used throughout the notes.

BIHR	*Bulletin of the Institute of Historical Research*
BJRL	*Bulletin of the John Rylands Library*
B.L.	British Library
BNYPL	*Bulletin of the New York Public Library*
CJ	*Journals of the House of Commons*
DNB	*Dictionary of National Biography*
EHR	*English Historical Review*
JHMAS	*Journal of the History of Medicine and Allied Sciences*
JPHS	*Journal of the Printing Historical Society*
JRSS	*Journal of the Royal Statistical Society*
MLN	*Modern Language Notes*
MLR	*Modern Language Review*
MP	*Modern Philology*
NQ	*Notes and Queries*
PBSA	*Papers of the Bibliographical Society of America*
PHIBB	Project for Historical Bio-Bibliography
PMLA	*Publications of the Modern Language Association*
P.R.O.	Public Record Office
R.O.	Record Office
SB	*Studies in Bibliography*
ser.	series
STC	A. W. Pollard and G. R. Redgrave. *A short-title catalogue of books printed in England, Scotland and Ireland . . . 1475–1640*. London, 1926. 2nd ed., revised by W. A. Jackson, F. S. Ferguson, and Katherine F. Pantzer, Vol. 2. London, 1976
TCBS	*Transactions of the Cambridge Bibliographical Society*
VCH	*The Victoria History of the Counties of England*
Wing	D. G. Wing. *Short-title catalogue of books printed in England, Scotland, Ireland, Wales, and British America . . . 1641–1700*. New York, 3 vols., 1945–51. 2nd ed., Vol. 1. New York, 1972

CHAPTER I

London and the Country

During the early months of 1695, both houses of Parliament devoted some time to the need to renew the Printing Act, which was due to expire at the end of the session. This legislation, in force since 1662 with a gap between 1679 and 1685, had replaced the earlier executive decrees for the control of the press.[1] It regulated many aspects of the book trade, with the overall effect of confining commercial printing, and hence publishing, to London. For over two centuries, the London trade had exercised a collective monopoly over the production of books in England, and although a number of bookshops existed in the provinces, they were dependent upon London suppliers. From the late sixteenth century onwards, there is copious evidence for the existence of a provincial book trade. There were indeed few towns of any size in which books were not available. Among the examples are a trader in Chester in 1593,[2] Christopher Hunt in Exeter from 1593,[3] and William Corbett of Newcastle-upon-Tyne who died in 1626.[4] Shops also existed in the two university towns, although these were, of course, wholly atypical of the trade as a whole. Even outside Oxford and Cambridge, however, there were some bookshops with substantial stocks. In 1644, John Awdley of Hull had well over two hundred books in stock, including a wide range of classical texts, schoolbooks, and theological works both learned and popular.[5] By the end of the century, even the record of imprints,[6] which is only the tip of the iceberg of the country trade, shows a wide spread of booksellers throughout the country.

The beginning of the eighteenth century nevertheless marks a distinctive change in the organisation of the provincial book trade, and indeed of the English book trade as a whole. Among the several unintended consequences of the lapse of the Printing (or Licensing) Act was the legalisation of provincial printing. The lapse of licensing, the most important event in the history of the English book trade between the chartering of the Stationers' Company in 1557 and the initiation of the Net Book Agreement in 1900, introduced a new factor

1

of great significance into the relationship between the London and provincial trades.

In 1695, there was no tradition of provincial printing. The existing provincial booksellers were unable, for lack of skill and equipment, to set up as printers even had they wished to do so; had they succeeded, they could hope for no more than small and uneconomic local markets for their books. Despite these handicaps, however, printing was introduced into a number of provincial towns by men trained in London. The Common Council of Bristol was uniquely enlightened when it resolved within a few weeks of the lapse of licensing that 'a printing house would be useful in several respects', and invited William Bonny to establish a business even though he was not a Freeman of the city.[7] He printed documents for the Corporation, as well as doing work for individual tradesmen. Within a few years, probably in November 1702, he started *The Bristol Post Boy*, the city's first newspaper.[8] In all of this, except the initial invitation, he was a precursor of the typical provincial printer of the next thirty years. He and his like, without intending it, were to transform the trade and create a whole new mechanism of distribution.[9]

THE LONDON TRADE AFTER 1695

The lapse of the Licensing Act was by no means an unmixed blessing for the London book trade; indeed they petitioned Parliament several times for its renewal. This was not because they were philosophically or politically committed to a controlled press; it was because they saw a free press as an economic catastrophe for themselves. Their primary concern was with copyrights, the crucial privilege of the sole right to print and publish a particular work. Such rights were traditionally established by entry in the Hall Book of the Stationers' Company, and entries were compulsory in law for so long as the Licensing Act was on the Statute Book. The lapse of the Act opened the door to a chaotic world in which copyrights could be protected only by long and costly suits in Chancery. The trade asked for a Licensing Act; what it really wanted was a Copyright Act, and this it obtained in 1710.[10]

Meanwhile, however, the trade had developed internal machinery for its own protection. The first was, in effect, a wholesaling system which ensured that popular books were distributed only by a small group of London booksellers. This group met regularly from the 1690s to hold private auctions at which books were sold wholesale for resale either direct to the public or to the provincial booksellers. The group was known as the 'Conger';[11] the conger system was highly effective, handling over 170,000 books, to the value of nearly £37,000, between 1695 and 1705.[12]

The second defence mechanism was in the central area of the trade's concern: copyright. This was the trade sale,[13] an auction which, like the meetings of the congers, was open only to invited booksellers. At these sales, copyrights, or shares in copyrights, were sold. Although the continuous series of auctions of which catalogues are extant did not begin until 1718, there is great similarity between these sales and the earlier sales of books, and some evidence that such sales were held well before 1718.[14] It has always been accepted that these sales were intended by the booksellers as a defence of their rights, but usually with the inference that the intention was to protect copyrights against infringement.[15] The evolution of the system in the years after 1695, however, suggests another reason for its rapid growth, and perhaps even for its institution. By selling copyrights only within their own circle, the leading London booksellers were able to defend their collective control of the most profitable part of the publishing trade. If this was indeed their objective, they were remarkably successful, for the system itself survived into the nineteenth century, and the dominance of London was never seriously endangered. Because all the largest firms in London were involved, it was impossible for an author to sell his copyright outside the group if his book was to have a reasonable chance of success. Once one of these men owned the copyright, it would be sold, either as a whole, or in shares, only to other members of the group. To make protection absolute, it was implicit that when a copyright owner died or left the trade his copyrights were offered to the other booksellers at a trade sale.

The leading London booksellers thus retained their control of two of the three essential elements of any successful publishing enterprise: copyrights and distribution. They also had uniquely easy access to the third: production facilities. The printers had long since lost the dominant position in the trade which they had established in the sixteenth century. Few were now involved in the publishing of books, but were instead commissioned by publishing booksellers to undertake specific jobs. A few printing houses, however, became large and heavily capitalised businesses. In 1730, for example, Tonson and Watts were employing about fifty men,[16] and, later in the century, Strahan, Richardson, Bowyer, and others all had firms as large or larger. The concentration of skill and capital in London, the consequence of 150 years of a legally enforced collective monopoly, was so great that there could be no real provincial competition. The chain of cause and effect was circular: the demand for book printing was largely confined to London because the London booksellers successfully retained their control of copyrights and distribution; only the London printers could produce books on a sufficiently large scale; hence the dominance of the London booksellers was further enhanced by the availability of production facilities.

The trade acted with remarkable solidarity in the aftermath of the lapse of licensing, and they achieved, with little difficulty, their principal objective: London remained the only significant centre of English publishing.

THE RELATIONSHIP BETWEEN THE LONDON AND COUNTRY TRADES

The organisational structure which had evolved under licensing, and its retention and indeed reinforcement after 1695, put the provincial booksellers into an essentially dependent relationship with the London trade. The Londoners were the sole source of supply of all the books they published, and often went to considerable trouble to ensure that the country booksellers did not become sharers in such books. The very understandable obsession with the copyright question which is the central issue in the history of the English book trade in the eighteenth century is indeed the best introduction to an understanding of the relationship between the London and country trades, for it was the determinant of the dependency of the latter upon the former.

A few shares in London copyrights did find their way into the country trade. Most copyrights held by the country booksellers had country origins, but there are isolated examples of London shares which are of some interest. Benjamin Collins of Salisbury was particularly active in this respect. He owned shares in *The Rambler*, *Pamela*, *Humphry Clinker*, and *The Vicar of Wakefield*. The first two he bought privately from William Strahan, but he was one of a group of booksellers who made the original purchase of their copyrights from Smollett and Goldsmith.[17] Collins was unique in the scale and importance of his shareholdings, but other country booksellers did engage in similar activities. When they did so, however, distance, and the exclusive attitudes of the London partners, often made for difficulties. Joseph Pote of Eton, who had close contacts with the London trade and was himself a Freeman of the Stationers' Company, experienced a tempestuous relationship with John Nourse, with whom he was joint owner of Bartlet's *Farriery*. Nourse actually had an edition printed without Pote's knowledge.[18]

Significantly, Collins had not bought his shares at trade sales, and it seems that this would have been almost impossible. In 1774, it was claimed by John Merrill of Cambridge that some country booksellers had tried to attend the sales, but had been expelled. Merrill was giving evidence to the House of Commons on a bill supported by the London booksellers but vigorously opposed by him and, according to Merrill, other country booksellers. According to the official report 'on cross examination, it appeared that they [the country booksellers] had been turned out for misdemeanours, for breaking the rules observed at sales, etc.', but the details are not given. The report is, in fact, biased in favour of the Londoners, and it seems likely that the substance of Merrill's evidence-in-chief was true.[19]

It was perhaps a little more common for the country booksellers to be shareholders in London periodicals and newspapers; this is not entirely surprising, for, as we shall see, country sales were even more important for these publications than they were for books. Collins owned a one-fourth share in *The Monthly Review*, which, after his death, was sold back to the other proprietors for £900.[20] He was also part owner of *The London Chronicle* and *The Public Ledger*.[21] James Fletcher of Oxford was a shareholder in *The Gazetteer* from about 1775 onwards,[22] and there may have been a few other examples.

In practice, publishing was not a major source of friction between the London and country trades, at least in the first half of the century, since there was no real possibility of country competition in major publishing enterprises, and little even of country participation. Towards the end of the century, however, we do find more country shareholding, largely achieved through copyright dealings, outside the trade sales, for which there is evidence from an early date.[23] By 1828, when the first surviving rules of the 'Principal Shareholders of Books' were written, it was accepted that there were country partners. Even then, however, their position was distinctly inferior, for, whether for reasons of distance or from some other cause, they were 'bound by the acts of the London partners'.[24] Their money was welcome; their opinions were not.

The reason for the greater participation by the country trade in the last quarter of the century was that after 1775 there was much greater freedom to reprint comparatively recent texts. In fact, the most difficult area of the relationship between the London and country trades until then had been in this area of reprinting, and, especially, of the reprinting and the selling of reprints of popular texts first published before the Copyright Act of 1710. This was a highly controversial subject, for, until the House of Lords finally decided against them in 1774, the London trade maintained that the 1710 Act merely confirmed common-law rights. They argued, in effect, that while the Act set a time limit on the specified statutory penalties for copyright infringement (as opposed to penalties in common law for the infringement of any rights of property), it did not limit the existence of the copyrights (or properties) themselves.[25] Under the Act, works already in existence on 1 April 1710 were protected for twenty-one years. On the London trade's interpretation of the law they were thereafter protected in perpetuity.

This was not, however, the only interpretation. In 1774, William Johnstone, giving evidence to the same committee as Merrill, told how he had tried to enforce his common-law rights as he saw them. He had, he said, threatened to take Chancery proceedings against Thomas Luckman of Coventry for printing *Pilgrim's Progress*, but had settled out of court. To agree to do so he had imposed Draconian conditions on Luckman: he was to hand over the offending books, pay Johnstone's expenses, and promise not to repeat the offence. Johnstone had entered the trade only in 1748, so the alleged offence had taken place after the statutory expiry of the Bunyan copyrights in 1732, and Luckman was exercising his rights under the 1710 Act.[26] In the whole forty-year struggle about the meaning of copyright law this is the only specific example quoted to Parliament of a threatened prosecution of an existing provincially printed book. It is not, however, the only example of interference in country publishing ventures. In 1757, John Baskerville of Birmingham was planning to print an edition of Milton, but, as he wrote to a friend, he was 'deterred by Mr. Tonson and Co. threatening me with a bill in Chancery if I attempt it'.[27] Tonson 'owned' the valuable Milton copyrights, and would not tolerate such 'piracy'.

Cases like this were very uncommon, but a continual source of irritation and disagreement was the related allegation that the country booksellers sold books illegally imported into England, in contravention of the 1710 Act and the further Act of 1739 which specifically forbade all book imports except of certain classes of learned works.[28] The 1710 Act applied only to England and Wales, and it was therefore legal to print in Scotland, Ireland, and the British possessions overseas, books which were copyright in England and Wales. It was, however, a breach of copyright to import such books into England and Wales for sale.[29]

There is a good deal of evidence that many such books were imported, and that in the north of England they were widely sold in booksellers' shops. In 1735, when the pre-1710 copyrights had expired, and the first batch of twenty-eight-year copyrights were about to lose their statutory protection, the London booksellers promoted a bill in Parliament to extend the term of years, and to strengthen the law against imports.[30] They claimed that their copyrights had been 'injured by Surreptitious Editions and Impressions made as well in Great Britain as in foreign parts',[31] but what their witnesses actually produced was evidence of the import and sale of Dutch and Irish reprints. Indeed, both from the evidence and from the Act which finally emerged in 1739 it is clear that this was their principal concern at that time.

Charles Rivington testified that he and Philip Miller had jointly published the latter's *Gardener's Dictionary* at £1.5s.od., but that an Irish edition had been sold in England for £1.2s.od.[32] He himself had bought a copy for that price from the shop of 'Mr. Hilliard', presumably Francis Hildyard,[33] in York. James Crockatt, another London bookseller, told the committee that he was present when a bookseller in Preston opened a parcel of books from Ireland, and from that parcel he had bought a copy of William Burdon's *The complete farrier*.[34] Two other booksellers then testified that Dutch reprints of English books had been imported and sold.[35]

The concerns of the London trade are clearly reflected in the 1739 Act. It is entitled 'An Act for Prohibiting the Importation of Books re-printed Abroad, and first composed or written, and printed in Great Britain'. Imports of such books were completely forbidden, under a penalty of the destruction of the books, and a fine of £5 plus twice the value of the books imposed on everyone involved in the transaction. The only exception, apart from learned works in classical and northern languages, was for books in existence in 1710 which had not been reprinted in England for twenty years, that is, since 1718.

The sale of foreign reprints, however, was not to be stopped by mere legislation. It is clear from the evidence already quoted that they were cheaper, that they were readily available at least in the north, and that the country booksellers continued to sell them. Twenty years later the London trade tried to take direct action against the country booksellers. On 23 April 1759, John Whiston, on behalf of the London trade, wrote to John Merrill of Cambridge, as a leading member of the country trade, to tell him that the Londoners proposed to prosecute booksellers who broke the provisions of the 1739 Act.[36] Whiston pointed out that he, Andrew Millar, James Fletcher of Oxford, and Merrill's own father, also a Cambridge bookseller, had already met and agreed to subscribe various sums so that they could buy at cost all the stocks of Scottish and Irish editions held by the country booksellers, and give them English editions in exchange. After 1 May, however, they proposed to prosecute any further offenders in the Court of Chancery.

Alexander Donaldson, fifteen years later, chose to interpret this letter as a threat, and so, in a sense, it was. Yet the threat was tempered with reason; in fact, the London booksellers, and their two country allies, were proposing to enforce the law at their own expense. Fletcher and Merrill, as the leading booksellers in the two provincial towns most profitable to the trade, were apparently happy to collaborate in order to maintain good relations with the Londoners. This is significant, for it shows that at least two members of the country trade recognised the need for such co-operation. Equally significant is the appearance for the first time of the Scottish printers, for it was they who were to be the main cause of concern during the next fifteen years.

Five days later, Whiston again wrote to Merrill, reiterating the points he had previously made. This time, however, he elaborated on the plan. 'Riders shall be appointed the first of May to inspect all the booksellers shops in England,' he wrote, and he then listed the names of thirty-two London booksellers, including all the leading members of the trade, who would jointly subscribe a total of £3,175 for this purpose (Donaldson, pp. 14–15). The sheer cost of the operation seems to have been the rock on which the scheme foundered, for it was not until November that a printed letter was generally circulated to the country trade explaining the intentions and motives of the Londoners; despite the earlier time limits, the offer to replace illegal books with London editions still stands (Donaldson, pp. 15–17). Donaldson regarded this letter as a 'masterpiece of low cunning';

certainly, it would have severely damaged his own trade in piracies if the plan had been carried out vigilantly.

As in the 1730s, the London trade was primarily concerned with imported books. There is passing reference in Whiston's second letter to 'pirated editions printed in England' (Donaldson, p. 13), but it was underselling by the Scottish and Irish imports which was the substance of the Londoners' concern. The problem, ironically, revolved largely around books already, by statute, in public domain, and when we consider how valuable they were we can see why the London booksellers were so worried that they subscribed over £3,000. Whiston had listed some of them in his first letter (Donaldson, p. 12):

The books will be mostly, I suppose, as follows: Spectators, Tatlers, Guardians, Shakespear, Gay's poems and fables, Swift's works, Temple's works, Prideaux's connection, Barrow's works, Rollin's ancient history, etc., Gil Blas, Whiston's Josephus, Burnet's theory, 2 vols, Young's works, Thomson's seasons, etc., Milton's poetical works, Parnell's poems, Hudibras, Waller's poems, Fable of the bees, 2 vols, Young's night-thoughts, Turkish spy, Travels of Cyrus.

All but three of these had no statutory protection,[37] but shares in them were still being sold at the trade sales, for all of them were constantly reprinted and highly profitable.

For another fifteen years the London booksellers fought to establish their view of the law. The battle coalesced over Donaldson, and it was *Millar* v. *Donaldson* which the Lords finally decided against the booksellers in 1774; with that decision the chimerical notion of perpetual common-law copyrights finally vanished.[38] Even then, the Londoners did not quite abandon their hopes. They petitioned the Commons for a Bill to overturn the Lords' decision, and the whole issue was aired yet again in a series of debates.[39] Merrill changed sides, and gave the evidence about trade sales already quoted; the Londoners testified to their plight if they lost the protection of the law; the letters of 1759 were discussed; and the Scottish and Irish pirates had their affairs dissected before a bemused House. It was here too that Johnstone's solitary and pathetic example of a country piracy was displayed. The Commons, more concerned with matters three thousand miles away, listened politely and dropped the bill.

Inevitably, these matters soured the relationship between the London and country trade from time to time, but never to the extent of causing a major breach. Indeed, moderation is apparent on both sides. In the well-documented events of 1759, two leading provincial booksellers played a crucial role on behalf of the London trade; the Londoners themselves moved very slowly, and with a considerable commitment of money to buy out rather than prosecute offenders. Perhaps a few country booksellers felt frustrated by the monopolistic attitudes of the London trade, but it is clear that some were admitted *de facto* into the magic circles at the heart of the trade. Some, like Luckman, were marginally inconvenienced by London booksellers choosing to stand on their alleged rights. Far more just sold the imports and hoped for the best. The moderation of the London trade, however, is best illustrated by considering that throughout this forty-year controversy they paid lip-service to the view that most country booksellers did not realise that they were selling illegal books. It can have been no more than lip-service, since the vast majority of the Irish and Scottish reprints have imprints which make no attempt to disguise their origins.

Why did the London trade hold back? Whatever the outcome of the cases on copyright, after 1738 they had the statute law on their side about imported English books, and yet except in 1759 they never really attempted to enforce it against the booksellers. One reason was certainly that they preferred, as far as possible, to deal with the problem at source, as in the prosecution of Donaldson. Equally important, however, was the impracticality of controlling the country trade. The 1759 exercise may have been a salutary warning; but it was far too expensive to become a permanent system of policing. Finally, there is the clear impression that the relationship between the London and country trades was slowly transformed into one of interdependence, because the growth of the provincial market for books meant that an ever-increasing percentage of a publisher's profit was derived from country sales. The Londoners could bypass the country booksellers only at great inconvenience to themselves, by dealing direct with provincial customers, and inherent in that was the danger that booksellers and customers alike would buy the imports of the most popular books if the London editions were not available.

So far, we have looked at the legal and structural relationship between the two sides of the trade. We have not yet considered their commercial dealings and the organisation of the distribution system. It is there that we shall find the key to an understanding of the comparative leniency of the London trade, and their reluctance to use the full rigour of the law. The fact is that during the first thirty years of the century, before the great copyright controversy started in 1732, the country trade had developed a highly effective distribution system of which the London booksellers were the principal beneficiaries. The remarkable growth of the country trade, and the growth within it of the distribution system which took books to the remotest corners of England, is the subject to which we shall now direct our attention.

CHAPTER 2

A Century of Growth

The legal and administrative structure of the trade is the framework
within which we must study its development. The history of that
structure also suggests chronological divisions. At the beginning of
the century, there were few printers and no newspapers in the provincial towns, but there were retailers with a long history of bookselling
and stationery dealing. By 1730 every large town had a printer and a
newspaper. The great copyright battle in the middle decades of the
century was largely a battle fought by the London trade to win and
retain the provincial market against the competition of Scottish, Irish,
Dutch, and, to a much lesser extent, provincial 'pirates'. Seen thus,
the battle had no decisive outcome; the London booksellers lost their
legal point, but not their trade. In the last quarter of the century,
the economy of England changed so profoundly that the old battles
became irrelevant. In a period of unprecedented growth there were
profits for everyone, and the book trade benefited as much as any
other.

The histories of the London and country trade are as inter-
dependent as were the trades themselves. If we periodise the history
of the trade in the eighteenth century, the periods 1695–c.1730,
c.1730–c.1775, and c.1775–c.1800 are applicable to both. Of course,
these divisions are not perfect, but they do offer a chronological
framework parallel to the developments in the legal and administrative framework, within which we can study the growth and
development of the trade.

THE ROOTS OF CHANGE: 1695–1730

The legalisation of printing and the establishment of a few presses did
not immediately change the nature of the existing provincial trade. At
the turn of the eighteenth century there were itinerant booksellers,
shopkeeping retailers, and some men who were both, all of whom
continued to pursue their affairs as they always had. Only gradually
did the presence of the printers begin to affect their activities, and

some, indeed, worked in the middle of the eighteenth century as their predecessors had done a hundred years before.

The itinerants were the first group to undergo change. The travelling bookseller was still a familiar figure at the beginning of the century, for although the practice is normally associated with the chapmen and balladsellers, who were little better than pedlars,[1] there were also itinerants who sold far more substantial books. The itinerant trade was an important element in the retail distributive system for many goods throughout the century,[2] and bookselling was only a partial exception. Michael Sparke, whose bevy of chapmen sold books in Bristol and along the Welsh border in the early seventeenth century, had a special reason for using such methods: he specialised in Catholic books.[3] Others, however, traded in less dangerous commodities. One of them was a Mr Haworth who, in 1692, was selling books in Bedford, Canterbury, Ipswich, Kettering, Kimbolton, Lutterworth, Northampton, Oundle, Uppingham, and Wellingborough (Map 1). Nothing is known of him beyond a single imprint, but, except for the rather surprising appearance of Canterbury and Ipswich in this list, he travelled among a group of market towns, all of which he could have covered on their market days in a fortnightly circuit.[4] Haworth, however, had few successors; bookselling became an occupation for shopkeepers, and the roads were left to the chapmen.

We do not know whether Haworth actually had a shop in any of the places where he worked, but there are many examples of booksellers who did combine the functions of shopkeeper and stallholder. The best known, for purely extraneous reasons, is Michael Johnson of Lichfield. His shop in Lichfield was, as we know from his son's account of it, well stocked. Some of his stock he sold at local markets, going as far afield as Ashby-de-la-Zouche, Birmingham, and Uttoxeter.[5] Johnson was not unique. Later in the century, John Clay of Daventry, Northamptonshire, had a stall, and later a shop, at Lutterworth, Leicestershire, and another in Rugby;[6] and there are many other examples.

The shopkeeper, whether he has a single shop or several, is clearly distinct from the itinerant whether he is a pedlar or a rather better-established trader like Haworth. The shopkeepers were always the majority in the book trade, and some firms existed for over a hundred years. The Dagnall family of Aylesbury, first recorded there in 1650, were still in business in the 1790s. At various times they also had shops

13

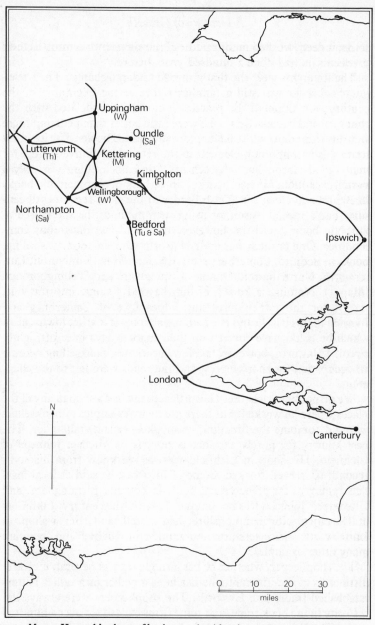

Map 1. Haworth's places of business, 1692 (showing roads and market days)

in Chesham and Leighton Buzzard.[7] The business was as profitable as it was long-lived. When Thomas Dagnall died in 1792 he left £2,000 in cash and stocks, and substantial properties in Aylesbury and elsewhere in Buckinghamshire, as well as the business.[8]

Johnson, Clay, and Dagnall were retailers, not producers, although both Clay and Dagnall operated small printing businesses at some of their branches later in the century. Johnson never printed at all. He occasionally published a book, as he did Sir John Floyer's *The prophecies of the Second Book of Esdras* (1721), but that, like the others, was printed in London. The shopkeeping retail booksellers were in the same relationship with the London trade as the country booksellers of a century earlier. They represented a development of the paper-distribution network which had established the initial contacts between members of the Stationers' Company and country tradesmen. For them printing was a mere sideline, if they did it at all; the arrival of the printing press in the provinces made no immediate difference to their mode of conducting business.

Obviously, the position was quite different for those who came into the country book trade as printers. Even here, there was something of a tradition of London booksellers setting up in the country. Christopher Hunt of Exeter (see p. 1, above) was a Freeman of the Stationers' Company;[9] in the 1590s, Roger Ward of Shrewsbury had a similar connection with London.[10] In the late seventeenth and early eighteenth centuries a number of Londoners moved into the country to establish their businesses. In 1681, John Barksdale went to Cirencester, and remained there until his death in 1718.[11] Obediah Smith, the founder of the business later owned by Clay, moved from London to Daventry in the mid-1680s, and his business, in his own hands and in those of his son, and of Clay and his son, survived until 1800.[12] Nevill Simmons, the son of a bookseller who had shops in both London and Kidderminster, established a shop in Sheffield in 1689, and was there until at least 1702.[13] These men may have had family connections with the towns where they chose to trade, but none is apparent in the cases of either Simmons or Smith, and the evidence is shaky in the case of Barksdale.[14] It seems at least as likely that they saw opportunities for developing a business away from the intense competition which characterised the London trade.

In one sense, therefore, the printers were following a well-trodden road. In another and more important sense they were pioneers. Bonny seems to have been the first provincial printer after the lapse of the

Licensing Act, but he was closely followed by Thomas Jones who established a printing house at Shrewsbury in the same year, 1695. Jones had been a printer in London, but he was a Welshman, and moved to Shrewsbury to print Welsh books and thus exploit the town's traditional role as an entrepôt for mid and north Wales.[15] In 1705 or 1706 he started a newspaper, *A collection of all the material news*, but it seems to have been short-lived and no copy is now extant.[16] The third provincial printer was probably Samuel Darker, who printed a volume of *Select hymns* in Exeter in 1698;[17] in the same year he went into partnership with Samuel Farley, and together, but with Farley as senior partner, they published *Sam. Farley's Exeter Post Man*, beginning perhaps in 1700, but more probably in 1704.[18] The next printer was Francis Burges of Norwich. He began to print on 27 September 1701, and a few weeks later he started *The Norwich Post*, almost certainly the first provincial newspaper.[19]

The stories of these pioneer printers have much in common. None was returning to his birthplace; Jones was the closest. All of them saw a gap in the market; this is implicit in Jones's Welsh printing, and explicit in the case of Burges.[20] Above all, they all published, or assisted others to publish, newspapers. Later country printers followed much the same pattern. James Abree, the first printer in Canterbury since the sixteenth century, set up his press in 1717, and immediately began to issue *The Kentish Post*. It was the foundation of a printing and bookselling business which made Abree a wealthy man by the time he died in 1768.[21] Samuel Hodgkinson, the first printer in Derby, and founder, in 1719, of *The Derby Post Man*, has a similar history.[22] John Bagnall left London immediately after completing his apprenticeship in 1720, and began to issue *The Ipswich Journal*; like Abree, he was the first printer in his town for nearly two hundred years. The firm which Bagnall founded survived, in various hands, until 1902.[23] These histories, and others, are almost tediously uniform.

The uniformity is suggestive in several respects. First, it suggests that there was a genuine demand for newspapers and that the distribution system of the London newspapers was not yet able to fulfil this demand. Secondly, it was a consequence of the related demand for local advertising media, a function in which the London papers could never wholly supersede the provincial press even when the distribution network was more highly developed in the second half of the century. Thirdly, it shows that a profitable business could be developed from such a newspaper. Finally, it emphasises the un-importance of book printing. Jones was a book printer, but he had a unique market. Darker experimented with book printing, but soon turned to newspapers. The others printed occasional books, but only after their presses were well established. The provincial printers were thus supplementing, rather than competing with, the London trade.

Newspaper printing in the first half of the century is the only aspect of the whole provincial trade which has been properly researched and analysed,[24] but it is important to recognise that it was only one part of a much larger whole. In the first thirty years of the century, when the newspapers were becoming a normal feature of provincial life, their proprietors relied heavily on existing booksellers in one important respect: sales. The printers could not hope to make profits on purely local sales. In fact, in order to do so they had to sell their papers over huge areas. In 1714, Henry Crossgrove wrote that his *Norwich Gazette* 'spreads all over Norfolk and Suffolk, Part of Lincolnshire and York-shire'.[25] This was not unusual. Robert Raikes and William Dicey, joint owners of *The Northampton Mercury*, claimed that their paper went 'further in length, than any other Country Newspaper in England, and takes in weekly the Counties of Bedford, Berks, Buck-ingham, Cambridge, Derby, Essex, Gloster, Hertford, Huntingdon, Leicester, Lincoln, Norfolk, Northampton, Nottingham, Oxford, Rutland, Stafford, Suffolk, and Warwick'.[26]

These claims can be checked by studying the geographical origin of the advertisements which were the only truly 'local' feature of the early provincial newspapers. The same issue of *The Northampton Mercury* had advertisements from Northampton itself, St Ives, Daventry, Loughborough, and Boston, and this is probably a more realistic reflection of the area in which it circulated in any quantity. Even so, it covered a good deal of ground. We should not, however, exaggerate the phenomenon. Edition sizes were small, probably no more than about 1,000 copies in the 1720s,[27] and the geographical spread of so small a number argues for limited demand, not the reverse. In order to achieve even this low level of economically necess-ary sales, and to increase the crucial advertising revenue, the printers needed agents in distant towns who would sell the newspapers and take in advertisements and subscriptions. It was at this point that the old trade of the stationers and booksellers and the new trade of the printers came into contact for the first time, to their great mutual advantage.

17

To illustrate this, let us take the same issue of *The Northampton Mercury*, and consider the four towns outside Northampton which were the source of advertisements. St Ives in Huntingdonshire was the town in which Raikes and Dicey had first established their press before going to Northampton; they were there in 1718–19, but retained their connections with the place after they left.[28] There had been a bookseller in Daventry since the 1680s, as we have seen, and we know that Clay was selling *The Northampton Mercury* in 1746, and probably much earlier.[29] There was almost certainly a bookseller in Loughborough by 1720; Matthew Unwin is recorded there in 1728, but he had been in the trade in the midlands since at least 1716.[30] In the fourth town, Boston, Lincolnshire, there was at least one bookseller, Henry Wilson, in 1720.[31] In other words, the towns in which *The Northampton Mercury* is known to have been available were towns which had a bookseller. Examples can be multiplied. In 1725, when *The York Courant* started publication, its agent in Hull and Beverley was Thomas Ryles, a well-established bookseller in both towns.[32] *The Weekly Courant*, published in Nottingham from 1712 onwards, was sold in Derby, York, Ashby-de-la-Zouche, and Chesterfield, and perhaps elsewhere, by established booksellers.[33] In 1720, *The Newcastle Courant* was sold by a number of booksellers in the north-east.[34] Other traders were agents for newspapers, but in most cases the majority were booksellers before they were agents. The newspapers, by 1730, had thus linked the old and the new in the provincial trade.

Professor Wiles has discussed the distribution system of the provincial newspapers at length;[35] the essence of it was that the papers were sold by agents, and that both agents and proprietors employed newsmen (or newsboys) who delivered the papers to subscribers. Hence there was a chain which linked proprietor, agent, newsman, and subscriber. As we have seen, many of the agents were established booksellers, but their agencies began to make a change in the way in which they conducted their businesses. Paper supply was the key factor. The newspaper owners were the largest provincial customers for printing paper. In the first decade of the century they had to buy this from importers and wholesalers, since there were no reliable local sources of supply on a sufficiently large scale. After 1710, the Stamp Act reinforced this dependence, for they were now legally obliged to buy stamped paper on which to print their newspapers. This was obtainable only from London. It was the need to obtain stamped paper which maintained the contacts between the newspaper owners and the London stationers long after paper was available from provincial mills, and hence with the London book trade as a whole. The same factor meant that the agents were, through the printers, able to gain regular access to London, as they had previously through the paper distributors. This was to be of great importance, for when English paper production reached a sufficiently high level to displace the reliance on imports, as it did in the 1730s, the country booksellers could retain their London links while exploiting the availability of cheap, regionally made paper. A dual system of supply, books from London and paper (other than that used for printing newspapers) from the provinces, was to be the next major development in the trade.

In 1730, there were about twenty provincial newspapers, of which about half had been in existence for ten or more years.[36] Among them they covered virtually the whole of England (Map 2). Each had supply chains of agents and newsmen, and were thus stimulating the development of the book trade in their circulation areas. This is one measure of the change wrought by the arrival of the printers. The provincial booksellers had, in less than thirty years, acquired a new role as newsagents, and the need for agents had created new bookshops. Because the newspaper owners made themselves a vital link in the chain of book supply, even agents who were not booksellers soon became deeply involved in the trade.[37] It was this which laid the foundations for the remarkable growth of the provincial trade in the next fifty years.

EXPANSION 1730–1775

The 1730s marked a turning point in the history of the English book trade in several important respects. First, there was the copyright issue, which came to the fore in 1732 with the expiry of the pre-1710 copyrights. Although there were other issues involved, it is clear from the events of 1759 and from other evidence that the retention of the provincial market was a significant part of the London trade's concern about this matter. Secondly, by the 1730s, the provincial newspapers were well established and provided ready access to the provinces, and the provincial booksellers, for both news and advertisements. Thirdly, in 1731, Edward Cave established *The Gentleman's Magazine*, the first periodical to command a large and truly national

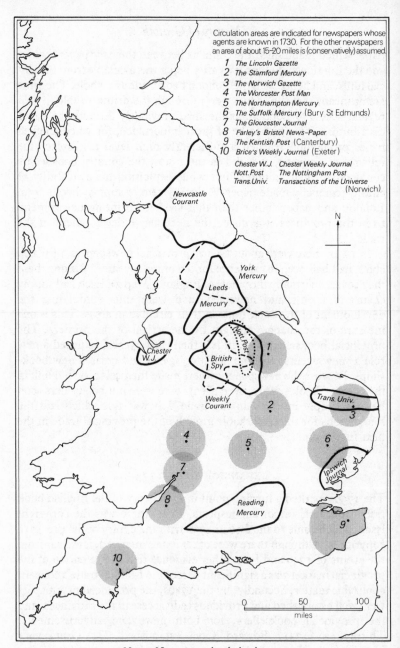

Circulation areas are indicated for newspapers whose agents are known in 1730. For the other newspapers an area of about 15–20 miles is (conservatively) assumed.

1   The Lincoln Gazette
2   The Stamford Mercury
3   The Norwich Gazette
4   The Worcester Post Man
5   The Northampton Mercury
6   The Suffolk Mercury (Bury St Edmunds)
7   The Gloucester Journal
8   Farley's Bristol News-Paper
9   The Kentish Post (Canterbury)
10 Brice's Weekly Journal (Exeter)

Chester W.J.   Chester Weekly Journal
Nott. Post   The Nottingham Post
Trans. Univ.   Transactions of the Universe
                              (Norwich)

N

Newcastle Courant

York Mercury

Leeds Mercury

Nott. Post

British Spy

Weekly Courant

Chester W.J.

Trans. Univ.

Ipswich Journal

Reading Mercury

0   50   100
            miles

Map 2. Newspaper circulation in 1730

market; Cave, with his provincial connections, was well aware of the importance of that market, and sought to exploit it, using the strategically placed printers like Dicey, Raikes, and Abree to help him.[38] Fourthly, it was in the 1730s that Robert Walker and others pioneered the cheap popular part-books, which were explicitly aimed at a provincial market, and like *The Gentleman's Magazine* sought to exploit the distribution networks of the provincial newspapers.[39] Finally, it was in the 1730s that the English paper industry was at last able to satisfy most needs, and imports fell sharply.[40]

From a provincial point of view, these developments, except for the copyright issue and paper supply, really represented the consolidation and confirmation of existing trends. Cave and Walker both made full use of the networks established by the newspaper owners as a means of penetrating the provincial market, Walker indeed combined the part-book and the newspaper, by using the former as inserts to the latter in a primitive form of syndication. Increasingly, the whole provincial trade came to revolve around the newspapers and their distribution, although the closely related stationery trade moved in a rather different direction. From the 1730s onwards more newspapers were established, so that by 1750 there were over forty, more than twice the number of ten years earlier. Circulation areas became more compact, but also more densely covered by networks of agents and newsmen. The tendency seems to have been to rely on agents in towns and newsmen in rural areas. In 1769, for example, the comparatively young *Leeds Mercury* had eighteen agents. Two were newsmen: one was based in Harrogate, and the other travelled Airedale and Wharfedale from a base at Malham. Of the others, all who can be traced were shopkeeping booksellers.[41]

Because of these developments, we can best understand the country trade in the middle of the century if we see it functioning on three levels: the newspaper owners; the newsagents; and the rest. The newspaper owners are the easiest group to study because through their papers they have left abundant evidence of their activities, but there is some information about all levels of the trade.

Thomas Slack of Newcastle-upon-Tyne began his newspaper, *The Newcastle Chronicle*, in 1764, a year after he left his former employer Isaac Thompson and set up his own press. His daughter, Sarah, married Solomon Hodgson, one of Slack's apprentices, a few months after her father's death in 1785. Sarah and her sister Elizabeth had inherited their father's business, and Hodgson was now in charge of it.[42] Later, he became friendly with Bewick, and published several of Bewick's books. Hodgson died in 1800; the business continued in the hands of his sons, Thomas and James, until 1849. By that time, James had been Mayor of Newcastle once, and was to hold the office again. It is an almost classic tale of the apprentice who married the master's daughter.[43]

William Jackson entered the trade in Oxford in 1746, as a partner with Walker, the part-book syndicator, in *The Oxford Weekly Flying Journal*. This paper lasted for only three years.[44] Six years later, Jackson tried again, this time more successfully, with *Jackson's Oxford Journal*, a paper which survived until after the First World War. The newspaper trade, however, was soon only one part of Jackson's activities. In 1780, he became the agent of the lessees of the Bible Side of the Oxford University Press,[45] and for eleven years after 1782 he was also the lessee of Wolvercote paper mill.[46] Later in life, he turned to banking, was the founder of the Old Bank (now a branch of Barclays) at Oxford, and when he died on 22 April 1795 he was a wealthy man.[47] Just how wealthy, we can judge from his will, made the day before his death.[48] He left over £13,000 in cash legacies to various friends and relations, as well as substantial properties in and around Oxford. Much of this may have come from banking; but it was his newspaper which had started him on the road to success.

Robert Goadby of Sherborne, Dorset, was another man who made a substantial fortune from a newspaper. Goadby entered the trade in 1744 at the age of twenty-three.[49] He was a Freeman of the Founders' Company of London but transferred to the Stationers' before 1757, and took several apprentices between that year and 1783.[50] He worked first in Yeovil, Somerset, where, probably on 1 July 1744, he began to issue *The Western Flying Post*. On 30 January 1749 he merged it with *The Sherborne Mercury*, formerly owned by Bettinson and Price,[51] retaining Goadby's original title. Goadby came to dominate a good part of the whole book trade in the west of England, for Sherborne was a strategic location from which to distribute books, and Goadby's newsmen were soon familiar figures throughout Somerset, Dorset, Devon, and Cornwall. Nichols described Goadby as 'a man of the utmost integrity and industry', adding that 'few men have been more generally known in the West than he'. He was also an author; he wrote a number of popular devotional works, and according to Nichols 'his publications were read by great numbers who scarcely ever read anything else'.

Like Hodgson and Jackson, Goadby had amassed a considerable fortune before his death in 1778.[52] A childless man, he bequeathed the business to his brother, Samuel, and his nephew, Samuel Lerpinière. The newspaper which was the basis of his wealth was entailed to their heirs. Family legacies amounted to about £2,500, to which have to be added family trusts producing £25 a year. This, however, was only the beginning. Goadby, true to his piety, left £200 in 3% Consols to the parish church; £2 a year was to be a fee for the vicar for delivering a sermon on the first Sunday in May on 'the Wisdom and Goodness of God in the Works of Creation', and the rest of the income was to be distributed among the poor of the parish. He also owned a half-share in an hotel at the fashionable resort of Weymouth; this was left to one Joanna Lee. His employees received £10 each, and his apprentices, of whom he had three at the time of his death, were to receive £5 each on attaining their freedom. These were the fruits of a substantial business which, except for the hotel, was entirely in the book trade.

These three men may be taken as typical of those who owned successful newspapers in the provincial towns; they were the financially stable and socially respectable proprietors of well-established and long-lasting businesses. In each case, the newspaper was the key to success. The network of agents and newsmen gave the newspaper owner unique access to the market in his hinterland, an access which was used not only for newspapers, but for periodicals, part-books, books, and many other goods and services.[53] The booksellers who were newsagents are thus a distinctive part of the trade, because they were beneficiaries of the success of the country newspapers. Indeed, the need for agents was instrumental in bringing men into the trade; at Ashbourne, Derbyshire, for example, the first bookseller was Thomas Hanworth, who established his business in 1721 as an agent for *The Derby Post Man*.[54]

For a more detailed example, we will take *The Reading Mercury*, founded in 1723 and bought by William Carnan in 1737.[55] Carnan had five agents outside Reading: A. Pote, Eton; 'Mr Ellott', Newbury; Judith Titheridge, Basingstoke; William 'Prier' (*recte* Prior), Winchester; and Edward Easton, Salisbury. Two of these, Ellott and Titheridge, are otherwise unknown, but the others either owned or were closely associated with prosperous bookselling businesses.

Easton was the most successful of them, although on a more modest scale than the newspaper proprietors whom we have discussed. He entered the trade before 1727,[56] and rapidly established good local connections. As soon as *The Gentleman's Magazine* began to be published Easton was supplying it to the Earl of Pembroke at nearby Wilton House, a connection which lasted for more than a century; his grandson, in 1830, rightly boasted of this record.[57] Easton died in 1753, leaving £400 in cash legacies, a good deal of property in Salisbury, part of which was worth £70 a year, and further property in Sutton, Wiltshire, which may have been his birthplace. His son, also Edward, was to inherit the business.[58] The second Edward Easton was 'eminent and respectable'.[59] In 1780, he was Mayor of Salisbury, and, like his brother James, he was also a magistrate in the city. He retired to Bradford-on-Avon, Wiltshire, in 1794, but died in February 1795 at the age of seventy-five. He was succeeded by his son, James, who, as we have seen, was well aware of the longevity of the business which he had inherited.

William Prior of Winchester is a more shadowy figure, but again we can detect a successful businessman and a respectable citizen. His agency for Carnan appears to be the first record of him; perhaps it brought him into the trade. In 1743, he was one of the two booksellers in Winchester who took subscriptions for *The Harleian Miscellany*;[60] in the following year his name appears in the imprint of a Winchester assize sermon.[61] The record of him is in fact very fragmentary, but this is, in a sense, why he is interesting. From these scraps of evidence we know only that he had a bookshop and was agent for a newspaper; neither Nichols nor Timperley saw fit to memorialise him. Yet he was sufficiently highly regarded in one of England's most ancient cities to be Mayor of Winchester in 1756.[62] This is a valuable warning. The retail booksellers, whether newsagents or not, have left few traces behind them, unlike the printers; this does not mean, however, that they were minor tradesmen of no importance, as Prior vividly illustrates.

A. Pote of Eton is something of a mystery. Joseph Pote was a famous bookseller in the town, as was his younger son after him. We have already met him as a shareholder in Bartlet's *Farriery*.[63] His son Thomas succeeded him on his death in 1787. It seems inconceivable that A. Pote was not related to Joseph; there is only one possible candidate, and that is his daughter Ann. Even she presents a problem. Her brother Thomas was apprenticed in 1748, when he was probably about sixteen.[64] She must have been substantially the elder of the two if she was in business on her own account as early as 1737, although she may have taken the agency in her own name as part of her father's business. On the other hand, we do know that there was a major division in the family. Joseph Pote had six children. In his will,[65] Thomas, the younger son, received the business, which he had run for several years; one daughter, Mary, was left a life interest in £250 in Consols; and two other daughters had £50 each. The two eldest children, James, a clergyman, and Ann, were cut off with 5s.od. each, because of their conduct. This conduct is not described, but clearly there had been a monumental quarrel. Is Ann's possible agency relevant to this quarrel? Did she assert her independence too much or too soon? We do not know, but the name is too uncommon for us not to suspect a link between A. Pote and Joseph, and that leaves us with Ann as the agent.[66] Whatever the ambiguities and uncertainties, we can again trace some kind of link between a newsagency and a significant provincial bookseller.

When we turn to the third level of the trade, the level of those who were not involved with the newspapers, we face a dilemma, for the range is very wide. John Clay, with his prosperous, locally oriented business largely dependent on sales of stationery for his profits, was probably typical.[67] Typicality, however, is a dangerous concept here, and only the study of scores of individuals like Clay could reveal it. Unfortunately, this is impossible, for it is only the fortuitous survival of Clay's business records which has rescued him from the oblivion which has engulfed most of his contemporaries. We can proceed only by taking a few examples and treating them individually.

John Hogben of Rye, Sussex, was in business from 1735 onwards; the firm passed to his son, also John, at an unknown date, and existed until at least 1786. Hogben was a bookseller, stationer, and bookbinder. He also sold maps and prints, globes, mathematical instruments, and spectacles. To all this he added the local agency for the Sun Fire Office, the sale of fishing tackle, and a private school of which he was Master. A mixture indeed, but for thirty years it supported a family.[68] The diversity of Hogben's business, save in the provision for anglers and schoolboys, was not exceptional.[69]

If Hogben is perhaps typical of the small traders who sold books and paper on a small scale in the middle of the eighteenth century, we must not ignore those who were at the other end of the spectrum. There had been well-stocked bookshops since the middle of the seventeenth century, and some of these shops continued to exist quite independently of the newspapers, while others were established. Samuel Mountfort in Worcester was such a bookseller during the middle decades of the eighteenth century. He was in business from 1725 until at least 1760.[70] In that year he advertised a stock of about a hundred named titles, and many more unnamed, both new and second-hand; the stock was diverse and impressive in both depth and range. In 1776, Ellen Feepound of Stafford had a stock of about two hundred books, very unlike Mountfort's.[71]

Robert Keymer of Hadleigh, Suffolk was a member of a bookselling family which had worked in the nearby town of Colchester since the middle of the seventeenth century. He was in business by 1750 at the latest, and probably earlier, for he died in 1776. He left a total of £570, as well as stock and his house; the house was worth £250.[72] Another tale of quiet prosperity is revealed by the will of Joseph Turner of Cirencester, Gloucestershire, who is first recorded in the mid-1730s, but who, like Keymer, may have been in the trade for much longer. He had £370 at his disposal when he made his will in 1748, and it was duly distributed after his death in 1754.[73]

Hogben, Mountfort, Feepound, Keymer and Turner may be taken to represent those who traded as their predecessors had done, benefiting from the growth of the provincial market, but not directly participating in the stimulation of that growth through the newspaper-based distribution network. They all sold books, and, for a few, books were an important part of their business, but they were also stationers and sellers of many other goods and services. They are perhaps too different from each other to be called a group within the trade, for they do not have the obvious common characteristics which link newspaper proprietors or newsagents. Yet there are similarities between them and they were, numerically, a significant group.

One common characteristic they do most certainly share: they were retailers, not producers. This differentiates them from another group whose emergence is a distinctive and important development in the trade in the middle of the century: the jobbing printers. All printers, including the newspaper proprietors, undertook some jobbing work; but whereas in 1730 virtually every printer had a newspaper, by 1775 this was no longer the case. Again, we can best proceed by example, starting with one of the best documented of all eighteenth-century provincial printers, John Cheney of Banbury, Oxfordshire.[74]

Cheney started life as an innkeeper, but in 1767 he became a printer. Although he was to build a reputation as a printer of ballads and chapbooks, he also did a great deal of jobbing work throughout his life, and jobbing was the most important part of his trade when he first went into business. Within three years, he was earning about £50 a year from printing, undertaking such jobs as advertising handbills, auction catalogues, blank forms for legal documents, and letterhead writing paper. Within a very short time the tradesmen of Banbury must have wondered how they had functioned at all when the nearest printer was twenty miles away in Oxford. Cheney left to his successors a well-established and prosperous business which continues to this day.

The country jobbing printers were often operating single-handed, or with help from their families or a couple of boys. Luke Hansard, later to achieve fame and immortality in a more glamorous part of the trade, was apprenticed to just such a printer in Norwich in the 1760s. Stephen White, Hansard's master, had learned his trade from Henry Crossgrove of *The Norwich Gazette*, and set up in business for himself in about 1760, when Hansard joined him.[75] According to Hansard's own account, he served White as 'compositor and pressman, corrector and manager, copperplate printer and shopman, book-keeper and accountant to this chequered business'.[76] Small firms like White's proliferated in the middle of the century in places as far apart as Lewes[77] and Liverpool.[78]

These printers produced the same sort of material as that printed by Cheney in Banbury, although those in the larger towns had the additional opportunity to print official documents for the Corporation. Municipal printing was, to some jobbing printers, a very important part of their work. In the 1760s and 1770s, for example, Joseph Heath, a Nottingham printer, printed a number of handbills, invitation cards, and similar documents for the City Council, of which he was a member.[79] Heath had a good business, established in the 1740s, and later expanded with a branch in Mansfield.[80] Similar work was done in Sheffield in 1747 by John Garnett, another printer without a newspaper.[81]

The expansion of the printing trade was a matter of comment by contemporaries. Samuel Johnson wrote in *The Idler* in 1758 that 'almost every large town has its weekly historian, who regularly circulates his periodical intelligence'.[82] Johnson was not alone in this observation. William Blackstone, two years earlier, had told the Delegates of the Oxford University Press that there was 'now hardly a Country Town of any name, but what furnishes one or more Printers'.[83] As early as 1746, however, Thomas Gent, himself a printer in York, had strikingly, if with slight exaggeration, compared the printing trade then with its state in 1724 when he had left London for the provinces. According to him, in 1724 there were 'few printers in England, except London . . . none then, I am sure, at Chester, Liverpool, Whitehaven, Preston, Kendal, and Leeds, as, for the most part, now abound'.[84]

The middle decades of the eighteenth century witnessed growth in all aspects of the provincial book trade. Newspapers proliferated, and most were successful. In their wake, they brought newsagents who were able to start or, more often, develop substantial bookselling businesses. Other booksellers and stationers, great and small, existed alongside the newsagents, and printing was fully integrated into provincial life so that jobbing work became a sufficient basis for a business. The picture is that of an expanding trade, and we can now understand why the Londoners were so concerned about the provincial market. A few, like Cave and Walker, exploited it with new kinds of publication. Others, longer established and heavily committed to investments in copyrights, sought to defend their markets against the incursions from abroad of which the provincial trade were the not unwilling intermediaries.

THE TRADE IN A CHANGING ECONOMY: 1775–1800

No area of business life was unaffected by the fundamental changes in the British economy which gathered momentum in the last quarter of the eighteenth century. The rapid development and vastly increased wealth of the newly industrialised cities like Birmingham and Manchester put tremendous strains on service provision of all kinds. Public services broke under this strain, but those which were provided commercially were significant beneficiaries of the new prosperity. Booksellers and stationers were small cogs in a large machine, but they were certainly not immune from the tides of change. In the last quarter of the century we find more of them, and larger firms; we find a distinct shift away from the south and east towards the industrial areas of the north and the midlands; and along with success we find failure of the sort associated with too rapid expansion in a volatile economy.

Quantification of the trade is a difficult exercise; it cannot be attempted with mathematical precision, but some approximations are possible. In 1700, we know of 97 traders in 41 towns, but these figures are certainly too low, for they are derived from sources which are at least partially incomplete.[85] We should probably double the number of traders, and increase the number of towns by about 25%. For the middle of the century, the best guide is the list of subscription agents for *The Harleian Miscellany*, which seems to have been more comprehensively marketed than almost any book of the century; this produces 381 traders in 174 towns in the mid-1740s.[86] Even allowing for inaccuracies and underestimates, this confirms the suggestion of notable growth.

The first directory of the trade, compiled by John Pendred in 1784–85, was not intended to be a complete list; it had a very specific purpose which provides invaluable evidence for the distribution system, but which is irrelevant here.[87] For the 1790s, however, we do have a reasonably comprehensive source, *The Universal British Directory*. This was the first real attempt at a complete list of traders in England and Wales, and although it has defects it is useful to us.[88] It records 988 firms engaged in various book trade activities in 316 towns (see Appendix IV). The real total of members of the trade may be about 1,100, plus a quite incalculable number of shopkeepers who sold a little stationery or a few schoolbooks in their general stores. Without straining the evidence we can detect a trend: the trade penetrated into more and smaller towns, and it did so markedly in the last few decades of the century. From the same sources, we can detect another trend; whereas in 1700 the centres of the provincial trade were cities like Cambridge, Canterbury, Exeter, Norwich, and Oxford, by 1800 they were Birmingham, Leeds, Liverpool, Manchester, and Worcester. In Leeds certainly, and elsewhere probably, the growth of the trade was not only absolute but also relative to the growth of other trades.[89]

Within individual cities we find similar trends. In Newcastle-upon-Tyne, where the history of the trade has been very thoroughly researched,[90] there were two firms in 1700, and between ten and fifteen in most years between 1736 and 1771. After that, growth was rapid: twenty-five in 1776, thirty in 1782, a peak of thirty-eight in 1787, and between thirty and thirty-five throughout the 1790s. In Bristol, there were thirty-three firms in 1775,[91] forty-two in 1793,[92] and in 1794 forty-five according to *The Universal British Directory*. In Liverpool, there were eleven firms in 1766, fourteen in 1774, and thirty-four listed in *The Universal British Directory*; by 1800 there were ninety-eight.[93] The growth of the trade in Newcastle and Liverpool, with the stimulus of their industrial hinterlands, was noticeably more marked than in the comparatively moribund city of Bristol, remote from the new industry.[94]

The shift towards the new centres of wealth and population is unsurprising; service industries go to their customers. Although the market for books and newspapers increased, the really dramatic growth was probably in the industrial and commercial market. The printing trade benefited by producing packaging, labels, and advertising materials. The stationers benefited from the vast demand for paper generated by large-scale industrial and commercial enterprises. No firm was wholly immune from the new trends; even in Banbury, distant as it was from manufacturing industry, Cheney increased his income from jobbing printing alone to almost £100 a year in the 1790s, twice that of thirty years earlier.

Along with expansion came over-expansion and failure. Formal bankruptcies were uncommon in the provincial book trade until the last quarter of the century. Firms were usually small family affairs, and the level of capitalisation was generally low. Between 1710 and 1769 only twenty-four members of the trade appeared in Chancery from this cause;[95] between 1770 and 1799 there were eighty-five. Bankruptcies in all areas of trade increased in the last three decades of the century, but more markedly so in the book trade. Over the whole period 1732–99, about 30% of all bankruptcies were between 1790 and 1799;[96] in the provincial book trade nearly 50% of bankruptcies were in that last decade. Over-expansion and over-optimism were the usual causes, and especially the failure of a new firm to compete against a longer-established rival. John Bayley of Ashford, Kent, will serve as one example; he failed in 1798,[97] unable to compete with Edward Pike in a town of only two thousand inhabitants.[98]

The picture, however, was not generally gloomy despite individual failures. William Tesseyman of York entered the trade in the 1760s, was 'many years a respectable book-seller',[99] retired, bought a country estate, and justifiably styled himself 'Gent'.[100] He was not alone; Abraham Brown, a successful Bristol bookseller, also called himself a gentleman.[101] So too did William Clachar of Chelmsford, Essex; he was a substantial landowner who in 1795 insured his property for £6,500, less than £2,000 of which was now connected with the book-trade activities which had made his fortune.[102] William Edwards of Halifax, Yorkshire, who is remembered as a binder, but who was the largest bookseller in a rapidly developing industrial town, had no less than £11,000 in Consols alone in 1807.[103] For the successful the rewards were great indeed.

From a small but solid base the provincial book trade both expanded and changed in the eighteenth century. In the first thirty years, the pioneer newspaper printers opened up the country to the trade through their agents and newsboys. Between 1730 and 1775 this achievement was consolidated and developed, against the background of the London trade's determination to penetrate and retain the potentially huge provincial market. In the last quarter of the century, the book trade, freed from restrictions, was a major beneficiary of general economic growth. Some of the successors of those pioneers became wealthy landowners and capitalists – not, it is true, on the scale of the ironmasters or the millowners, but substantial businessmen nevertheless. All of this depended upon the availability and accessibility of the market, and it is to that market that we shall now direct our attention.

CHAPTER 3

The Market for Books

In the year 1700, the city of Norwich, the first provincial town to have its own newspaper, was the largest town in England after London. It was the centre of the wool trade, England's greatest industry, when that trade was reaching the peak of the development shortly to be hymned by Daniel Defoe. It was not only in economic terms that Norwich dominated its hinterland. It was also the social focus of Norfolk for the gentry and the prosperous farmers; there was a social season with balls, concerts, and plays. Within the city there was a growing number and proportion of professional men and of traders who, like Francis Burges, were providing services. Norwich was both the prototype and the archetype of the pre-industrial city which was to reach its fullest point of development in the next fifty years.[1]

During the first half of the eighteenth century, we can distinguish between the regional capitals, like Norwich, and the lesser market towns. The first group were of social and political, as well as economic, significance. They were, for the most part, county towns, and hence the seat of the Assizes and the site of elections. Elections and Assizes, and associated social events such as race meetings and assemblies, brought the gentry to town. At the same time, the increased demand for services made the regional capitals into service centres, providing the means to meet the financial, legal, and medical needs of the surrounding rural communities. In the rich farmlands of the south and east, cities like Winchester, Leicester, and Canterbury followed the pattern established by Norwich. The lesser towns were local entrepôts. They had regular markets which attracted both buyers and sellers, and their tradesmen included a few who acted as small-scale wholesalers to shopkeepers in even smaller places. This established pattern of the urban economy was disturbed by the rise of the industrial cities, but it remained constant even then in the areas not directly affected by industrialisation. The book trade, despite its elaborate distribution system, was no exception to the general pattern of trading life.[2]

Within the provincial towns and the surrounding countryside were

32

those who actually bought the books, magazines, and newspapers which the booksellers sought to sell. It is notoriously difficult to define a market, and even now surveys can produce little more than generalisations about the class and income structure of the book-buying public. For the past, the difficulties are even greater, and the results even more nebulous. Yet we must try to paint at least the broad outlines of a picture of the book buyers, and of the books which we know they bought and read, before we can understand why the country book trade expanded so greatly during the eighteenth century. Underlying the picture is the expansion of the economy, beginning, it ought to be remembered, in the countryside, not in the towns, and the rapid growth in the population after about 1740. We can, however, be a little more precise than this, and consider both books and book buyers in a number of categories, to gain some understanding of the customers who patronised the booksellers' shops which were so comparatively rare in 1700 and so common a hundred years later.

THE EDUCATIONAL MARKET

An educated public is the basis of a successful book trade, and not the least important reason for the expansion of the trade during the eighteenth century was that education was itself a growth industry. The provincial newspapers are full of advertisements for schools and academies of all kinds. The schoolmasters may have left something to be desired; we can, perhaps, doubt the mathematical proficiency of John Hogben, the Rye bookseller (p. 25 above). Yet despite what were often low standards, there was a marked rise in the rate of basic literacy, until it reached perhaps 75% among urban men by the end of the century.[3] In other words, the ability to read had spread far down the social scale, and although the working man's hold on literacy may have been tenuous, it did nevertheless create a market for educational books, and for cheap and simple leisure reading later in life.[4] From the charity schools at the beginning of the century to the Sunday Schools at the end, there was a continuous tradition of philanthropic education for the poor, which ensured that England entered her industrial revolution with a remarkably literate population despite the absence of state-aided public education of any kind.

The dame schools and charity schools used few books, yet there were so many of them that their text-books were among the best-

33

selling books of the century. The London printer Charles Ackers printed thirty-three editions of Thomas Dyche's *A guide to the English tongue* between 1733 and 1747, a total of some 265,000 copies, or nearly 18,000 copies a year,[5] of which a mere handful is extant.[6] Sales on this scale, which were a direct consequence of the growth of elementary education, were a major source of revenue to all booksellers. The largest category of books in Ellen Feepound's shop in Stafford in 1776 was 'about 140 Books for Scholars in English and Latin'.[7]

Booksellers' advertisements and other sources throughout the century show the same preponderance of school books. In 1730, Thomas Hammond of York advertised his stock, beginning with 'Bibles, Prayer-Books, School-Books. . . .' (cf. Plate 3 on p. 76, below);[8] thirty-seven years later, Patrick Sanderson of Durham gave similar prominence to the same parts of his stock.[9] A handbill issued by Cheney, probably in 1788,[10] follows the same pattern:

Bibles, Testaments and Common Prayer Books, Dictionaries, Spelling Books and Reading made Easy's . . .

Reading made easy, like Dyche's *Guide*, was printed in tens of thousands; Clay bought copies by the hundred from J. W. Piercy of Coventry in the 1770s.[11]

Elementary education in reading and writing, using English as its teaching medium, was by far the most common form of schooling in the eighteenth century. At a higher level we have to distinguish between classical and modern education, although the two overlapped in the dissenting academies. The academies[12] were probably the best schools in England. They had their origin in the need to circumvent the Anglican grammar schools and universities, but they gained so good a reputation that they were able to attract pupils from outside the ranks of the nonconformists. Their curricula were only partly classical; they taught modern languages and literatures, history, geography, mathematics, and, in the true tradition of English dissent, commercial subjects. Above all, they were the only educational institutions in which science was taken seriously; Joseph Priestley was a tutor at Warrington Academy when he first made his name as a chemist. In Daventry, Clay made a good deal of profit from selling books to both pupils and masters at Ashworth's academy, which was in the town for most of his career.[13] William Eyres, a Warrington bookseller, made a substantial fortune from selling books to members of the Academy there, and added to it by becoming one of the few provincial publishers of any importance, issuing a number of works written by the tutors and their friends.[14] The academies, vigorous and innovative, were a major source of revenue for their local booksellers.

The old grammar schools, with their purely classical curricula, were less important to the book trade, not least because many suffered from falling rolls. Some schools, however, did flourish. It was during the eighteenth century that Eton surpassed Winchester and established itself as England's leading school.[15] The business of Joseph Pote was one of the beneficiaries of Eton's new prestige. It was, however, in the very antithesis of the ancient foundations that the most lively potential book market was to be found: in the technical and commercial academies.

There were hundreds of such academies during the century, ranging from the great institutions of dissent to men who taught a little accounting or bookkeeping in their own homes.[16] Hogben was not unique among booksellers in running such a school, or among schoolmasters in selling books. *The Universal British Directory* tells us of two more: Thomas Palmer of East Grinstead, Sussex, was Master of a school there, and William Perks of Bath was a writing master and accountant as well as a stationer. In Leicester, two booksellers were also schoolkeepers: Richard Phillips, and Isaac Cockshaw, both in the 1790s.[17] Mathematical education, and training in mathematically based technologies such as surveying and navigation, was the basis of education in these little schools. Books on these subjects continued to proliferate, and were marketed widely throughout the century.[18]

THE PRACTICAL MARKET

There was some degree of national uniformity in the educational market. Although there were regional trends, like the origin of the Sunday School movement in Gloucestershire and Somerset, the pattern from Durham to Daventry was generally similar. When we turn to the market for practical books, and even more when we consider leisure reading, local variation is more apparent. We shall, however, begin with one category of uniform national interest: the law. Law books were not only for lawyers. The gentlemen–amateurs who maintained the king's peace from the local bench were among the most important customers for legal publications. Giles Jacob wrote

35

prolifically for them, producing such works as *The complete parish officer's guide* and *The complete court-keeper*. Copies tend to be rare, and it is difficult to compile a full record of the bibliographical history of these works, but *The complete court-keeper*, for example, a handbook for manorial stewards, went through at least six editions in the fifty years after its publication in 1713.[19] Books on land law, conveyancing, the law of trespass, and the game laws were everywhere in demand, both by the justices and by their fellow landowners, while the clergy provided a ready market for works on the law of tithes. Law books, like school books, are ubiquitous in the booksellers' catalogues and advertisements.

The law and its practitioners impinged on the trade from another direction. Lawyers were among the best customers of both the stationers and the jobbing printers. Clay made about a quarter of all his sales to Thomas Caldecott, the Recorder of Daventry, who was the town's leading attorney. He sold him paper, ink, pens, and sheets of vellum, as well as printed forms.[20] The involvement of the trade in the sale of duty stamps further enmeshed it in dealing in law stationery.[21] The printers also benefited. Between 1794 and 1800 Cheney printed documents to the value of nearly £100 for two Banbury attorneys; this represented nearly one-fifth of his total income from jobbing work, and the demands of the lawyers were exceeded only by those of the auctioneers.[22]

The part-books, aimed as they were at a provincial audience, included many practical books. Indeed, among the very earliest of them was Joseph Moxon's *Mechanick exercises, or The doctrine of handyworks* (1678–93), now remembered as the first technical description of printing in English, but in fact a far-ranging instructional manual.[23] Later part-books included G. Bird's *Practical scrivener* (1733), Joseph Champion's *Practical arithmetick* (1733), Elizabeth Blackwell's *Curious herbal* (1737), James Dodson's *Antilogarithmic canon* (1740), John Tacker's *Art of cookery* (1746), and many more.[24] From the counting house to the kitchen the scope was very wide, and the same variety is found among works published complete as it is among the part-books. Instructional works of this kind were aimed at more than a purely professional market. The apprentice and the housewife, the gardener and the builder, could all learn or improve their skills from the printed word. In a complex and competitive society such books were in great demand. Among the century's most improbable best-sellers was Batty Langley's *City and country builder's and workman's treasury of designs* (1740), which popularised the classical style which we now call Georgian, and was instrumental in creating the new townscapes of Blandford, Newcastle-upon-Tyne, and Bath.

The newspapers should also be mentioned here, for they too had a practical purpose. The early provincial newspapers did little more than reprint news from their London contemporaries a week or so after its original publication. Even editorial opinions were usually taken from the same source, for not until the 1790s do we find provincial editors beginning to take an independent line.[25] The local appeal of the provincial newspapers was based on their advertisements, not on their news coverage.[26] It was as an advertising medium that the provincial press came to play a crucial role in social and economic life. Goods and services were offered in profusion; employers sought employees, and the unemployed advertised for work. In fact, the increasingly dominant advertising pages of a mid-eighteenth-century provincial newspaper were very like those of its modern successor. The proprietors were able to use their papers and their networks of agents to advertise and to sell a wide range of goods. This was particularly important in the book trade itself, but had a far wider significance in making the local newspapers an integral part of both urban and rural life.

The provincial papers gradually became more local in orientation, because by the middle of the century the London papers were easy to obtain in the provinces.[27] In the first thirty years of the century, only a few thousand newspapers were sent into the provinces; the total circulation figures of a London weekly reached 10,000 only in the most exceptional circumstances of war or political crisis.[28] A growing percentage of these copies went into the country; in 1722 provincial sales of *The London Journal* amounted to 650 copies a week, but by 1726 the number rose to 2,200.[29] The provincial market continued to expand, until by 1796, 23,500 newspapers a day, or over $8\frac{1}{2}$ million a year, were leaving London.[30]

This huge traffic was largely independent of the book trade, since it was the Post Office which undertook the distribution of newspapers. In fact, it provided a very substantial part of the income both of the Post Office itself and of some of its senior officials, and led to a number of practices which were verging on corruption.[31] Even though it was the Post Masters rather than the booksellers who dealt in London newspapers, the trade did nevertheless benefit from their availability.

The transformation of the London press into a national press by the middle of the eighteenth century provided, for the first time, a national advertising medium, supplementing advertising in local papers. This had profound consequences for the trade (pp. 47–50 below). Moreover, it allowed the provincial papers to develop into truly local news media. It is also a striking testimony to the existence of a large, literate, knowledge-hungry and news-seeking public in the second half of the century.

THE RELIGIOUS MARKET

The popular image of the eighteenth century as a time of official ecclesiastical torpor and philosophic doubt or indifference is belied by the unceasing flow of religious literature. If the Church of England bestirred itself only to quarrel about Sacheverell or Hoadley, dissent flourished, and Methodism gave renewed strength to the religious life of the provinces. In the north, the midlands, and the west country, the Church lost the towns to the Methodists, and they, like all dissenters, emphasised a personal relationship with God achieved through private reading and devotion. The sales of Bibles and of devotional works never fell away, and Methodist books were to become a significant part of provincial publishing.[32] For every Gibbon, there were thousands of devoted followers of Wesley seeking salvation through literacy. Long before Wesley began to preach, however, Bible-based protestantism had provided an important source of trade for the booksellers. This was as true in the eighteenth century as it had been in the sixteenth. In the single year of 1733, there were part-book editions of Burkitt's *Expository notes on the New Testament*, Burnet's *History of the reformation*, Court and Lindsay's edition of the New Testament, Foxe's *Book of martyrs*, Harry Lyndar's *A book of martyrs the best preservative against popery*, the Stackhouse's *New history of the Holy Bible*.[33]

Although the clergy were a major group of book buyers, it was their congregations which made the religious market so important. Most of those part-books were for the pious layman, not for his priest. There were many others. *The Christian pattern*, a translation of the *Imitatio Christi*, by George Stanhope, Dean of Canterbury, which had first been published in 1698, went through more than twenty editions in thirty years, and in the 1720s was still a valuable and much-traded copyright.[34] The same author's version of the liturgical epistles and gospels had an even longer history of success; Clay, Mountfort, Feepound, and hundreds of other booksellers stocked it for most of the century.

James Lackington, the pioneer of remainder bookselling, is a valuable witness to provincial reading habits in the middle of the century, even if he occasionally exaggerated for literary effect.[35] There is indeed some exaggeration in his account of his own early library, assembled in Bristol in the late 1760s, but it gives a flavour of the tastes of the religious book buyer in the provinces:

We all worked very hard, particularly Mr. John Jones and me, in order to get money to purchase books; and for some months every shilling we could spare was laid out at old bookshops, stalls, &c. insomuch that in a short time we had what *we* called a very good library. This choice collection consisted of Polhil on precious Faith; Polhil on the Deliverance; Shepherd's sound Believer; Bunyan's Pilgrim's Progress; Bunyan's Good News for the vilest of Sinners; Bunyan's Heavenly Footman; his Grace abounding to the chief of Sinners; his Life and Death of Mr. *Badman*; his Holy War in the town of *Mansoul*; Harvey's Meditations; Harvey's Dialogues; Rogers's Seven Helps to Heaven; Hall's Jacob's Ladder; Divine breathings of a devout Soul; Adams on the second epistle of Peter; Adams's Sermon on the *black* Devil, the *white* Devil, &c. &c. Colling's Divine Cordial for the Soul; Pearse's Soul's Espousal to Christ; Erskine's Gospel Sonnets; The Death of Abel; The Faith of God's Elect; Manton on the Epistle of St. James; Pamble's Works; Baxter's Shove for a *heavy-arsed* Christian; his Call to the Unconverted; Mary Magdelen's Funeral Tears; Mrs. Moore's Evidences for Heaven; Mead's Almost a Christian; The Three Steps to Heaven; Brooks on Assurance; God's Revenge against Murder; Heaven upon Earth; The Pathway to Heaven; Wilcox's Guide to eternal Glory; Derham's Unsearchable Riches of Christ; his Exposition of Revelation; Alleine's Sure Guide to Heaven; The Sincere Convert; Watson's Heaven taken by storm; Heaven's vengeance; Wall's None but Christ; Aristotle's Masterpiece; Coles on God's Sovereignty; Charnock on Providence; Young's Short and sure Guide to Salvation; Wesley's Sermons, Journals, Tracts, &c. and others of the same description.[36]

The rising comedy, and the juxtaposition of genuine and false titles, does not disguise Lackington's point.

Elsewhere in the *Memoirs*, Lackington gives a more objective account of a country tradesman's library. His colourful career had included a spell as an apprentice to a shoemaker in Taunton, where his unfortunate master was George Bowden, an Anabaptist. Bowden had a few books but, except for William Foot's *Practical discourse concerning baptism* (1739), they do not show any particular sectarian bias:

ster's whole library consisted of a school-size Bible, Watt's Psalms and
s, Foot's Tract on Baptism, Culpepper's Herbal, The History of the
Craft, an old imperfect volume of Receipts in Physic, Surgery, &c. and
Ready Reckoner.[37]

Watts's *Hymns and spiritual songs* became a staple soon after its
publication in 1707, joining *Pilgrim's Progress* as a work often produced by provincial printers in a chapbook format.[38] The rapid
increase in literacy, and the closely related growth of protestant
fundamentalism, among small traders and labourers in town and
country alike, provided a good income for the provincial book
trade.

THE LEISURE MARKET

From schoolboys to bishops those who read of necessity also read for
pleasure. In Clay's accounts, there is a rare and welcome touch of
humanity when Master Watts, a pupil at the Academy, spends sixpence on *The history of little Tommy Trip* to sweeten the pill of Corderius and Bayley.[39] Reading for pleasure was widespread among all
classes, so much so that it became a matter of contemporary comment.
Johnson wrote that 'All foreigners remark, that the knowledge of the
common people of England is greater than that of any other vulgar.'[40]
One of these foreigners was a man whose agreement Johnson rarely
welcomed or obtained; Voltaire had noticed that 'C'est que l'état
mitoyen est plus riche et plus instruit en Angleterre qu'en France.'[41] A
great deal of evidence suggests that reading was a popular and even a
fashionable pastime. The development of the novel after the 1740s
gave a greater impulsion to an existing trend; Lydia Languish's
circulating-library novels were as delightful to her as they were hor-
rifying to her future father-in-law.

The novel was, until the early nineteenth century, an upper- and
middle-class vogue; among a much wider range of readers a long time
passed before it displaced the older stories, half history and half
legend, which were the subject of the chapbooks and ballad sheets.
Both these last were printed in millions. Because even the great
factories of Bow and Aldermary Churchyards could not meet the
demand, chapbooks were printed throughout England.[42] The elder
Dicey continued to print them at Northampton long after his son had
moved to London; Newcastle-upon-Tyne was a major centre of production; Cheney became famous for printing them; from Clay's

records we know that several printers in Coventry specialised in producing them.[43] The ubiquity of chapbooks and ballads is apparent everywhere in the country trade. They were by far the most common form of printed matter throughout provincial England. Almost every advertisement has a note to the effect that these 'Histories' or 'Penny Histories' were in stock. The sheer quantity of production is sufficient evidence of a vast market. In the 1790s, Hannah More paid the chapbooks the compliment of imitation in trying to attract a mass audience to her Cheap Repository Tracts. Her complaints about the 'multitudes of the lowest rabble [who] . . . purchase these execrable tracts' [the chapbooks],[44] and the 'vulgar and indecent penny books . . . brought down to the pockets and capacities of the poor'[45] are further witnesses to the continuing appeal of the chapbooks.

Leisure reading was not, of course, confined to chapbooks, or indeed to fiction. The books stocked by the booksellers, to be considered in Chapter 5, are one guide to literary tastes, but another important indicator is in the holdings of the circulating libraries and book clubs. Circulating libraries, as commercial enterprises, were stocked with books which met a popular demand. By the end of the century such libraries were widespread; in 1801 it was estimated that there were 'not less than one thousand' of them.[46] This is so close to the estimated number of bookshops (p. 29 above) that it is tempting to suggest that there were few bookshops which did not include a small lending library. Ellen Feepound, for example, had 'about thirty books in the Circulating Library', and again many advertisements suggest that a library was a normal part of any bookseller's trade.

There are few surviving catalogues of provincial circulating libraries, but these few suggest that the smaller ones, like Feepound's, were largely made up of fiction. In 1790, Michael Heavisides of Darlington, County Durham, had a library of 466 works, of which all but about 50 were novels. At the other end of the scale, however, novels represented only about 5% of Ann Ireland's stock of nearly 2,500 books at her library in Leicester in 1789.

The average stockholding of fiction was about 40%, a figure which suggests a high demand for comparatively serious reading matter.[47] The book clubs and proprietary libraries, which in the nature of their organisation closely reflected the tastes of their members, have an even more striking bias towards non-fiction. At Ely, for example, the

Pamphlet Club bought only 29 novels out of 147 identifiable books between 1766 and 1776.[48] A similar pattern is found at other clubs of which some details are known, such as those at Cirencester, Fairford, and Bibury in Gloucestershire,[49] and at Clavering, Essex, in the 1780s.[50]

In the great urban proprietary libraries, which became an important feature of provincial culture in the last quarter of the century, the demand for serious literature is even more apparent.[51] With holdings running into thousands, against the few score books in the club libraries, they had only a small percentage of novels,[52] for in one library at least, that at Bristol, the interests of the members were chiefly in history, antiquities, and travel books.[53] We shall find similar fashions reflected in booksellers' catalogues, and can take the book clubs and proprietary libraries as a reasonably accurate reflection of the leisure market for serious literature.

Who actually used the libraries? The familiar image of the well-bred lady and her maid reading the latest pulp fiction is parody rather than reality. The much-satirised libraries of Bath did indeed cater for these women, but even Marshall's great emporium there, probably the largest commercial library outside London, had a majority of male members, and a stock of which nine-tenths was non-fiction.[54] More typical were the tradesmen and clergy of Ely who came together in the Pamphlet Club, and the worthy citizens of Bristol.[55] These people, and the members of similar institutions elsewhere, were precisely those who could afford to buy books, newspapers, and magazines, and they represented the core of the market for the stockholding bookseller. The pattern is not significantly different from that which obtains in England today; book buying was essentially a middle- and upper-class pursuit, in which a small minority of the population made a disproportionate number of purchases.

The steady increase in the price of books after about 1780, and the ever-growing number of books published, impelled this group towards borrowing rather than purchase, or at least to supplement purchases with borrowing, and also impelled the movement towards collaborative purchase. Their tastes for historical, geographical, and political literature, leavened with a little fiction, remained constant whether they were in the bookshop or the library. The leisure market expanded during the century because the classes who constituted it, the so-called urban gentry of wealthy merchants and professional men, were an increasingly conspicuous feature of the social structure of the provincial towns.[56] It was this class which made some booksellers rich; reading for edification, instruction, and pleasure, they were the market which the London trade was so anxious to retain through its control of the production and distribution of books.

CHAPTER 4

The Distribution System

The size of the provincial market, and its rapid expansion, were among the most compelling reasons why the London trade defended their historic position so vigorously. Their success, however, would have been in vain if they had been unable to supply that market. The failure of the London chapbook printers to retain their national market, exemplified by the vast provincial production of chapbooks, could have been an augury for the whole trade. It is true that for less popular literature the changeless economics of printing worked in favour of the Londoners; demand may have been national, but it was limited, so that for many books a single print run of 2,000 copies could satisfy the entire demand. On the other hand, to justify such print runs, and hence to achieve the cost benefits of mass-production, the London publishers had to reach a non-metropolitan audience as well as their local customers. This chapter investigates that process, central to an understanding of the country book trade. We shall follow a book from its publication and marketing to its arrival in the provincial shop, and seek to answer five basic questions. How did the provincials, booksellers and book buyers alike, discover what books were available? How and from whom were such books ordered, and on what terms were they supplied? Was there any mechanism for the central supply of books through wholesalers or others? How were books actually transported, and at whose expense? And, finally, how did books reach the country bookshops and their customers?

ADVERTISING

Advertising is the key to the widespread marketing of any product; books were, and are, no exception. Four advertising media were used by the trade in the eighteenth century: lists of books in print; newspapers; catalogues; and prospectuses. Book advertising is almost as old as printing itself, but only gradually did it become common. Lists of the works of an individual author were issued in England at least as early as 1561; the advertising of books in newspapers began in 1626;

44

an English publisher first issued a catalogue of his own publications in 1649. The latter practice was surprisingly uncommon until late in the eighteenth century, at least as a separate document; publishers' 'catalogues' were more often printed on a few blank leaves at the end of a book.[1]

The lists of books in print were the first major marketing development in the English book trade. The pioneer was Andrew Maunsell in 1595, but the first general list was William London's *Catalogue of the most vendible books in England* (1657), which was followed by the long series which began publication in 1668, with John Starkey's *Mercurius librarius*. This series, retrospective to 1668, is known as the *Term Catalogues*.[2] The *Term Catalogues* were issued quarterly at the end of each legal Term from 1668 to 1709, and cumulated four times in 1673, 1675, 1680, and 1696.

The explicit purpose of these catalogues was to make known what books were available, particularly to customers with no direct access to the London bookshops. William London was a bookseller in Newcastle-upon-Tyne; although little is known about him, his large *Catalogue* which he claimed to be of books 'All to be sold . . . at his Shop in New-Castle' supports the suggestion that he had the largest stock in the north of England.[3] London, however, had a rather wider intention than is normally implied by a bookseller's catalogue of his stock. He dedicated *A catalogue* 'To the Wise, Learned and Studious in the Northern Counties of Northumberland, B^{ppk} of Durham, Westmerland and Cumberland' (A3^r), and in the Epistle to the Reader he explained that he tried to compile a comprehensive catalogue of books which 'are to my own knowledg usually sold in most places of repute in the Country' (c1^r) for the benefit of the inhabitants of the four counties. He then devotes 49 pages to 'An introduction to the use of books in a short essay upon the value and benefits of learning and knowledge' (c3^r-13^r), which perhaps suggests that the wise, learned, and studious were not very numerous north of the Lune and the Tees.

This was a provincial enterprise, but it may have influenced Starkey and Clavell. In his preface to the 1696 cumulation, Clavell wrote (A2^r):

It is in the Interest of all the *Booksellers* in *England* to have this *General Catalogue* in their Shops; and those Gentlemen that buy it that live at some distance from their Booksellers, it would be convenient when they give Commission for any, to mention who they are, or were Printed for, then when such Orders reach *London* they might be got with the more ease.

The *Term Catalogues* were intended for the public as well as for the trade, but Clavell assumed that orders for books would reach London through the country booksellers. It was a dual purpose which such lists of books in print have always retained. The last of them in the early eighteenth century was John Worrall's *Annual catalogue*, which was published only in 1737 and 1738. In 1737, Worrall wrote in his preface:

The following LIST was principally intended, for those Gentlemen, Ladies, &c. who live remote from *London*, or seldom see the Multitude of News-Papers, wherein Books are advertised; that they might for a small Expence see what BOOKS have been publish'd in the Preceeding Year *1736*.

In 1738, to make his catalogue 'more Compleat and Useful', Worrall added a list of the names and addresses of London booksellers so that orders could be properly directed, just as Clavell had emphasised the need 'to mention who they are, or were Printed for'. This vital clue to the distribution system will be discussed later (pp. 59–62).

Worrall's second catalogue was destined to be his last, for by the late 1730s the separately published catalogue of books in print had been temporarily superseded by a particularly attractive competitor. Such a catalogue was not revived until 1760 when there appeared *A complete catalogue of modern books*, ancestor of *The London catalogue* (1773–1855), *The English catalogue* (1853–1968), and *The British National Bibliography* (from 1950).

The competitor arose out of the periodical catalogues themselves. In 1714, the London bookseller Bernard Lintot issued the first *Monthly Catalogue* of books newly published; this survived only until 1717, but John Wilford revived the name and the format in 1723. Five years later, *The Monthly Chronicle*, founded in January 1728, began to print lists of books preceded by extracts from the month's news, a formula adopted with great success by Edward Cave when he started *The Gentleman's Magazine* in 1731.[4] In March 1730, *The Monthly Catalogue* and *The Monthly Chronicle* merged under the latter title; in March 1732, under the stimulus of competition from Cave, the title was changed to *The London Magazine*. There now began a period of intense rivalry between the two magazines which forced Cave to abandon his former practice of culling his book lists only from the newspapers, and instead to seek information directly from the publishers. This they supplied because Cave's magazine was so patently successful and popular, and the new accuracy of the book lists became in its turn an important point in its favour for its readers.[5]

Cave could, moreover, offer one great advantage to the trade: he carefully and successfully cultivated the country circulation of *The Gentleman's Magazine*, utilising the contacts he had made in the provinces when he had acted as London correspondent of *The Gloucester Journal*, *The Stamford Mercury*, *The Kentish Post*, *The Northampton Mercury*, and perhaps other newspapers, in the mid-1720s.[6] As a consequence, *The Gentleman's Magazine* achieved a very wide circulation and was able to perform the functions of *The Monthly Catalogue* and its predecessors as efficiently as they, but more agreeably, and to a much wider circle of readers.

These catalogues, whether published separately or in the magazines, also helped to ensure that the London monopoly remained intact. By the middle of the seventeenth century there had been a need, expressed and fulfilled by London and Clavell, to provide information about current books for the country booksellers and their customers. Clavell, Wilford, and Lintot were all important members of the London trade; both Clavell and Lintot were substantially involved in the activities of the wholesaling conger as suppliers, and Clavell subscribed to multiple copies of Clarendon's *History* of 1704.[7] They were aware of the need to preserve the monopoly of the London trade as a whole, and one way of helping to do this was to ensure that those living outside London knew what books were available. The formula which Wilford discovered and Cave perfected ensured a wide circulation of lists of new publications without even the expense of advertisements. The monthly lists thus became an integral part of the trade, reaching their full development in the crucial decade of the 1730s when they were instrumental in enabling the leading London booksellers to expand and consolidate the achievements of the previous thirty years.

Newspaper advertising also became an important part of the system at about the same time. The newspapers were well established in London by the beginning of the eighteenth century; the first permanent daily, *The Daily Courant*, appeared in 1702, although for some years thrice-weekly publication remained common, on Tuesday, Thursday, and Saturday, the nights on which mail left London for the principal provincial towns. The integration of the newspapers into provincial life has been discussed (pp. 37–38, above); in 1721, the circulation of one weekly newspaper, *The London Journal*, had reached 10,000 copies per issue.[8] Although this was exceptional, it shows a vast increase over 1712, when only two newspapers, the thrice-weekly *Post Boy* and *Post Man*, exceeded 3,000.[9] Book advertisements are a feature of all eighteenth-century newspapers; they included the publisher's name, and the names and addresses of the booksellers from whom the book could be obtained.

Although some newspapers, like *The St. James's Chronicle* and *The World*, were aimed at a specifically London readership, the great majority regarded country circulation as an important factor in their financial arrangements. This was especially true of the evening newspapers.[10] The proprietors of *The General Evening Post*, between 1770 and 1785, were continuously concerned with co-ordinating their publication time with the departure of the Post Office mail coaches to the provinces. They paid the Clerks of the Road 'as a recompense for their extra trouble', which included holding back the coaches when the paper was delayed, and sending letters from their country correspondents ahead of the main delivery of letters.[11] The London newspapers, especially the country-oriented evening newspapers, were consequently ideal for advertising products such as books distributed by a single producer and his nominated agents. Many newspaper publishers were also book publishers, but they were sometimes willing to accept advertising from any publisher who wished to buy space. The ready availability of a national advertising medium was another factor in enabling the London booksellers to maintain their control of the trade.

The book advertisements for a single but typical month exemplify this. In January 1780, 268 titles were advertised in four London and five provincial papers; in all there were 876 book advertisements.[12] Of the 268 books, however, fewer than 8% were advertised only in the provinces, and fewer than 6% in both the London and provincial newspapers. The five country papers were all widely circulated in their respective areas, but the London newspapers were obviously regarded as the most satisfactory advertising medium. This is confirmed when we consider the books advertised only in the provinces. It is unsurprising that *Charges to Grand Juries delivered at the Quarter Sessions of the Peace for the County of Worcester* was advertised only locally (*BWJ*, 4466 (20 Jan. 1780)), or that Jean Claude's *An essay on the composition of a sermon*, in an English translation, is found only in *The Cambridge Chronicle and Journal* (900 (22 Jan. 1780)), whose proprietor Francis Hodson, was also the printer of the book. The twenty-seventh edition of *The Newcastle memorandum book*, published by Thomas Slack in Newcastle-upon-Tyne, was advertised in *The*

York Courant, but in none of the other selected newspapers (*YC*, 1831 (4 Jan. 1780)). It was an almanac and diary, of which there were many equivalents in London. In one or two cases the absence of a London advertisement may be pure chance. Three of John Fawcett's books were advertised in *The Leeds Mercury* on 4 January 1780, and two of them subsequently in *The Morning Chronicle* on 26 January. Fawcett was a Baptist minister at Hebden Bridge near Halifax; his considerable fame as a preacher and divine spread beyond the West Riding. and there is no obvious reason why the second edition of his *Advice to youth* should have been advertised in Leeds but not in London.[13]

Of the remaining books advertised only in the country, seven were legal works, and most of them concerned those aspects of the law which most closely impinged upon the country gentleman with land and a seat on the bench: the duties of a Justice of the Peace,[14] land law,[15] the game laws,[16] and tithes.[17] In addition, there are four religious works, all written either by evangelicals or by dissenters. In short, the books advertised only in the country are those which appealed primarily to country readers.

The books advertised in both London and the country are somewhat different from those advertised only in the provincial press, although there are some similarities; there are, for example, three legal works of the same class as those advertised only in the country.[18] On the other hand, at least three of the works advertised were of general interest, and appear to have been the subjects of something akin to national advertising campaigns. Such a campaign was no doubt necessary for the special *Form of prayer* prescribed for the General Fast held on 4 February 1780 as a supplication for much-needed divine assistance in the conduct of the American War. This was the most widely advertised publication of the month; there are thirty-nine advertisements for it shared among all nine newspapers. A similar campaign is discernible for *The modern universal British traveller* by Charles Burlington, David Llewellyn Rees, and Alexander Murray, published in weekly parts in 1779 and 1780. It was advertised widely in both London and the country; it is found in seven of the nine newspapers, and there are at least five different prospectuses for it in different forms.[19]

The third book was Charlotte Cowley's *Ladies history of England*, also published in parts and completed in 1780, which was advertised in eight of the newspapers, although no separate prospectus appears to be known.[20] Periodicals were advertised on the same basis, although

49

not as widely as Burlington or Cowley. Four new periodicals appeared in January 1780, and three of them, *The Political Magazine* (1780–91), *The Scourge* (1780), and *Shakespeare, a new periodical weekly paper* (which, if it was published, can no longer be traced), were widely advertised; the exception was *The novelist's magazine*.[21] There were also advertisements for the current issue of *The Westminster Magazine*.[22] Established periodicals seldom advertised, even in the London newspapers; there is one each for *The Gentleman's Magazine* (*LC* (31 Jan. 1780)) and *The London Review* (*StJC*, 2935 (1 Jan. 1780)); and two for *The Universal Magazine* (*LChron*, 3602 (1 Jan. 1780), and *StJC*, 2935 (1 Jan. 1780)). All the other periodicals which were advertised were in some way exceptional: *The Annual Register*, *The Parliamentary Register*, and *The Remembrancer*. The latter was edited by John Almon, and advertised only in his own *London Courant*. Apart from these, the only advertisements for periodicals were for the annual supplements of *The Lady's Magazine*, *The London Magazine* (in this case called 'The Appendix'), *The Town and Country Magazine*, and *The Universal Magazine*. No pattern can be found in the other works advertised both in London and the country; they include two works by John Fawcett, a book published at York and one published at Exeter, and a volume of *Trials for adultery*.

It is apparent that by the second half of the century at the latest the London newspapers were sufficiently widely circulated in the country to serve as the normal advertising medium for books. Only in exceptional cases, usually when a local author or subject was involved, or when the publisher was pursuing a particularly vigorous campaign to launch a new part-book or periodical, was there a real attempt made to advertise in the country newspapers. Even this was only for emphasis; it was the wide circulation of the London newspapers which ensured that information about new books was spread both widely and rapidly.

The book lists in the magazines and the advertisements in the newspapers provided a guide to new publications, but the former were neutral and the latter inevitably favourable. A more critical approach began to emerge in the middle of the century, with the foundation of Ralph Griffiths's *Monthly Review* in 1749, and of Smollett's *Critical Review* in 1756.[23] Smollett and his fellow contributors were particularly notable for their attempt to maintain a high standard of reviewing, and to criticise an author's writings rather than his political or religious opinions.[24] These periodicals were widely read outside

London, and became very influential in helping provincial customers to choose their books. The members of the Ely Pamphlet Club, for example, subscribed to *The Monthly Review* from 1766 to 1769, and to *The Critical Review* in 1775 and 1776, and used them as an aid in book selection.[25]

The third means of dissemination of knowledge about books, the publisher's catalogue, was still comparatively unimportant in the eighteenth century, but the importance of booksellers' catalogues grew rapidly. In the early eighteenth century, prices were not printed in the catalogue, but catalogues with printed prices began to appear in about 1730; the earliest extant example is that of the sale of the stock of John Darby, a London bookseller, on 7 February 1732,[26] although there seems to have been such a catalogue as early as 1729. By 1740 the practice was almost universal.[27] It is easy to understand why the printing of prices was so rapidly and generally adopted. Formerly, the potential customer for a book had to discover the price before placing his order; for the country customer this could be very time-consuming and expensive. The advent of the catalogue with printed prices was therefore greatly to the advantage of the customer distant from London, and one reason for its introduction was the convenience of provincial purchasers. The members of the trade themselves consti-tuted a substantial proportion of such customers; by the 1730s they represented a sufficiently important element in the trade as a whole to be instrumental in enforcing this change on the London booksellers.

The bookseller's catalogue, like the review, the newspaper adver-tisement, and the list of books in print, was concerned with books which were available, or about to become available within a very short time, at most a few weeks. The prospectus, on the other hand, was originally designed to persuade a customer to pay for his book before it was printed, or even before it was written. The practice of publication by subscription, preceded by the issue of a prospectus, began in England in 1610, when John Minsheu issued a prospectus for his Γλωσσον 'Ετυμολογικον, and after a slow start it grew rapidly to become the normal form of publication for certain classes of book, especially learned works.[28] By the middle of the eighteenth century the country trade was deeply involved in the publication of books by subscription. Minsheu seems to have made a tour to collect country subscribers in 1618 and 1619,[29] but a century later, with the spread of bookselling through the provinces, such methods became unnecess-ary.

An example will illustrate the extent to which the leading country booksellers became involved in subscription publication. The prospectus for John Glen King's *The rites and ceremonies of the Greek church in Russia* was issued on 1 January 1771.[30] It lists nine London booksellers, four of whom appear in the imprint of the book, and fourteen country traders. They were widely scattered through England, excepting the midlands and the north-west. This scatter is partly related to the author: born in Norfolk in 1732, he was a Cambridge graduate, spent many years as Chaplain to the English factory in St Petersburg, and returned to England as Rector of Wormley in Hertfordshire, a living to which he was collated in 1783.[31] It also, however, reflects the nature of the book: a learned work of ecclesiology, it would find its market in the universities and cathedral closes. None of the country booksellers is in the imprint, and since there is no list of subscribers, we do not know how far the publishers were successful in reaching the customers at whom they were aiming.

The part which the country booksellers played in such publications is clear from other books. William Betham was Head Master of an endowed grammar school at Stonham Market, about seven miles north of Ipswich. The prospectus for his *Genealogical table of the sovereigns of the world* was issued in March 1795 (Bodleian Library, Oxford. J. Pros. 397), and the book itself was published later in the same year. There were six London firms in the prospectus, and eight provincial booksellers in six towns. These are Deck, in Bury St Edmunds; Deighton, and Lunn, in Cambridge; Kelham, in Chelmsford and Colchester; Bush, Foster, and Jermyn, in Ipswich; and Fletcher, in Oxford. None of the country names appears in the imprint, and, except for Fletcher, they were clearly intended to ensure that customers who knew, or knew of, Betham on his home territory should have no difficulty in obtaining the book. In fact, Deighton, Foster, Jermyn, and Lunn appear in the list of subscribers, all except Lunn taking one copy only; Lunn took three.

In the case of Betham's book only those booksellers who were subscription agents subscribed, but this was not always so. Thomas Birch's edition of the *Thurloe State Papers* was advertised in a prospectus dated 4 December 1739 (Bodleian Library, Oxford. J. Pros. 86), and published with a list of subscribers in 1742. There are six London names in the prospectus, three of whom appear in the imprint of the book, one of them, Fletcher Gyles, posthumously; there are also eight country booksellers in as many towns, together with two in Dublin and Edinburgh, none of whom is in the imprint. Of the eight English booksellers outside London, only one, Martin Bryson of Newcastle, subscribed; he took three copies. Four other country booksellers also appear in the list, including Frederick of Bath and a second Newcastle bookseller. It may be that the others took no orders, but it seems more likely that they merely acted as agents, and that their customers appeared in the list of subscribers under their own names.

Although this explains why booksellers' names do not appear in subscription lists, it does not explain why they do. William Pryce's *Mineralogia Cornubiensis* provides a clue to this. Pryce lived at Redruth, and naturally his book was readily available in the west; one of the agents in the prospectus is the otherwise unrecorded T. Moor of Helston who was possibly a general shopkeeper acting as agent for a local book on this occasion.[32] Only five of the twenty country booksellers took copies in their own names, but five others appear who are not in the prospectus, all but one of them, Calcott of Banbury, in towns where another bookseller had been named as agent. Of these nine, only Sotheran of York, who took eight copies, and Goadby in Sherborne, who took four, can conceivably have been buying for stock; the others were acting as agents for customers. The three London booksellers also acted as agents, and were joined, or superseded, in that role by three others.

We can conclude that the country names in prospectuses are those of agents through whom subscriptions could be sent to the publisher or, as frequently happened with such books, the author, but that all booksellers were able to undertake this agency function. Why certain booksellers were selected by the publishers will be discussed later (pp. 64–68). The prospectus, itself advertised in the newspapers, was thus another means of publicising books over a wide geographical area, but it also ensured that books of local, but otherwise limited, interest were available in their own localities. Prospectuses merged into advertisements, and performed the same function in a slightly different way for a different kind of book: it ensured their availability outside London, and thus it also helped to maintain the dominance of the London trade.

ORDERING AND TRADE TERMS

A common feature in lists of current books, advertisements, and prospectuses is the prominence given to the names of the booksellers responsible for the book, and their country agents. As early as the end of the seventeenth century, Clavell assumed that country customers would order through their booksellers, and as the number of book-shops increased this assumption became steadily more realistic. The booksellers were in contact with the London trade, and could hence act as intermediaries between customer and publisher. The larger shops were distinguished by their substantial and wide-ranging stocks, but all booksellers, large and small alike, could order individual books for customers.

A bookseller would even act as an agent when a customer was buying from another bookseller. In 1781, Clay ordered fourteen books from a catalogue issued by James Robson of New Bond Street, London, on behalf of James Hitchcock, Vicar of Bitteswell, Leicestershire.[33] Hitchcock was a serious book collector who was a boon to Clay's trade. He had taken his B.A. from Pembroke College, Cambridge, in 1751, and was ordained in 1754;[34] in 1762 he was presented to the living of Bitteswell, which he held until his death in 1789. He had a reputation as a wit, but his talents as a parish priest can best be assessed from the fact that the more devout of his parishioners became dissenters. A neighbouring clergyman told Nichols that he was 'a literal Bookworm' and a man of great learning, although he had wasted his talents. Hitchcock's books were sold after his death to a bookseller in Leicester, who offered them at such low prices that almost all were bought by the London trade.[35] There were compara-tively few buyers like Hitchcock, but it is significant that one who bought books seriously and regularly considered his local bookseller to be the best intermediary, and did not always deal directly with the London trade.

Book orders are common in the few surviving letters from country booksellers to their London contacts. Another Leicestershire book-seller, William Harrod of Market Harborough,[36] was even willing to flatter John Nichols to expedite the order:

Squire Nevill of Holt tells my Daughter that he thinks you are a very clever Gentleman; and has ordered her to procure him:
1 Copy of your *Gartree* hundred, only, in boards.
You will therefore be pleased to forward me a Copy.[37]

There is also evidence for ordering of multiple copies of more popular books:

I was duly favoured with yours of the 7th Instant, & also with 50 Copies of our Good Friend in Barringtons New Register Books.[38]

Ordering books, however, was only the first stage of the process; payment was also necessary. The larger booksellers had London bank accounts on which they could draw. It seems that two months was the normal period of credit; Thomas Combe of Leicester drafted what amounted to a begging letter when he wanted three months instead.[39] Collins paid for his Register Books by 'a draft on Staple & C° at 21 days for £17.30–0',[40] but life was not always so simple, and, according to Lackington, 'many in the country found it difficult to remit small sums that are below Banker's notes'.[41] The banking system was fragmented, and could not be otherwise under the provisions of the Bubble Act of 1720. Bills and letters of credit passed back and forth, and one especial problem was that drafts drawn on smaller country banks were not always negotiable in London.[42] One solution was to have a London agent; John Albin of Newport, Isle of Wight, was fortunate in having a brother in London who could deal with his London bills,[43] but many other traders had greater difficulty.

For the country retailer, the discount he was allowed on the retail price was the key to the profitability of bookselling. Some dealings, especially when a large number of books was involved, were on a sale-or-return basis. At times this came close to making the bookseller into little more than a passive agent for the publisher. In 1773, Kincaid and Bell, publishers in Edinburgh, wrote to William Charnley of Newcastle-upon-Tyne 'desiring to know what Books he had disposed of and what are on hand and to send ye state of them p^r Course of Post'.[44] Two years earlier, they had been even more abrupt with him: 'The other Books you may keep until Summer and endeavour to dispose of what you can.'[45] In the newspaper trade sale or return was the normal basis of business; the proprietors of *The Gazetteer* gave full credit for return to William Meyler, their agent in Bath in the 1780s.[46] Sale or return could create problems. James Easton of Salisbury approached this delicate subject with caution, when writing to John Nichols: 'I beg to trouble you with my little account, having been standing for some years, and shall thank you for your Returns at your Convenience.'[47]

Discounts were an even more contentious subject, especially towards the end of the century when Lackington's activities began to disturb the equilibrium of the trade. There were, however, some accepted conventions. Harrod referred to 'the customary Allowance',[48] and Daniel Prince of Oxford felt obliged to apologise to Richard Gough for the unusually high price he charged for an edition of Polybius imported from Germany, but 'such are the German Terms'.[49] In general, everyone publishing books conformed with the usual English practices, even an author publishing his own work at his own expense. When Samuel Dunn issued his own *Epitome of practical navigation* in 1777, he had this notice printed opposite the title-page:

Mr. DUNN, Author of this Work, now resides in Maiden-Lane Covent-Garden, LONDON; opposite to a Book-binder's. His Mathematical Works, neatly bound, may be had of him, and by the Trade with the usual Allowance to sell again.

For the retail bookseller, 'the usual Allowance to sell again' was the source of his livelihood.

The classic description of 'the usual Allowance' is that by Samuel Johnson in a letter to Nathan Wetherall, Vice-Chancellor of Oxford University, written in 1776. The University was facing the problem, which had persisted since Fell's day, of persuading a London bookseller to act as agent for books published by the University Press. Johnson assumes that the Press will deliver its books to one bookseller, Cadel, who will warehouse them for the wholesaler, Dilly; Dilly will then sell them to the country bookseller. He continued:[50]

It is perhaps not considered through how many hands a Book often passes, before it comes into those of the reader, or what part of the profit each hand must retain as a motive for transmitting it to the next . . .

The deduction I am afraid will appear very great. But let it be considered before it is refused. We must allow for profit between thirty and thirty five per cent, between six and seven shillings in the pound, that is for every book which costs the last buyer twenty shillings we must charge Mr. Cadel with something less than fourteen. We must set the copies at fourteen shillings and superadd what is called the quarterly book or for every hundred books so charged we must deliver a hundred and four.

The profit will then stand thus. Mr. Cadel who runs no hazard and gives no credit will be paid for warehouse room and attendance by a shilling profit on each Book, and his chance of the quarterly Books.

Mr. Dilly who buys the Book for fifteen shillings and who will expect the quarterly book if he takes five and twenty will sell it to his country customer at sixteen and sixpence by which at the hazard of loss and the certainty of long credit, he gains the regular profit of ten per cent. which is expected in the wholesale trade.

The Country Bookseller buying at sixteen and sixpence and commonly trusting a considerable time to gain but three and sixpence, and if he trusts a year, not much more than two and sixpence, otherwise than as he may perhaps take as long credit as he gives.

With less profit than this, and more you see he cannot have, the Country Bookseller cannot live; for his receipts are small, and his debts sometimes bad.

Johnson's account of the discounts is summarised in Diagram 1. By these criteria, the country bookseller was given a discount of about $17\frac{1}{2}$% on the retail price, from which, of course, he had to cover his costs as well as make a profit. Allowing for the quarterly copies, Cadel has 1s.0d. in the pound, and Dilly 10%, each to cover both costs and profit. Johnson was accurately reflecting the practices of the trade, but we have to take account of the fact that he was writing about provincially published books whose publisher had a London agent. For London books, we can make slight adjustments (Diagrams 2 and 3). In Diagram 2 the book passes from publisher to wholesaler to retailer, and in Diagram 3 it passes direct from publisher to bookseller, taking as the base Johnson's assumption that the publisher will charge 70% of the retail price to his immediate customer, whether wholesaler or retailer. If a wholesaler was used, his profit came out of the bookseller's discount; generally, however, the country bookseller could expect between $17\frac{1}{2}$% and 30%, a range which, with an increased lower limit, was still the practice in the nineteenth century until discounts were effectively controlled and to some extent standardised by the Net Book Agreement.[51] The whole issue was further complicated by the variable price of books which was a consequence of simultaneous issue in different forms of binding. There were, however, more or less fixed prices for each form; prices are often quoted for 'sheets', 'stitched', 'wrappers', or 'boards'. The 'usual Allowance' was made on the basis of the price for a particular form of binding.

We can now turn to an actual example which will illustrate the system at work. In 1795, William Edwards of Halifax wrote to Thomas Hood in London to complain about the price he had charged for a copy of John Aikin's *Description of the country from thirty to forty miles around Manchester*.[52] Hood had charged £2.15s.0d.; the retail price of the book was £3.3s.0d.[53] Edwards had previously obtained a copy from another bookseller for £2.12s.6d. 'and no Commis.[n] to pay which makes a Material difference when Carridge is added'. Hood's price had reduced Edwards's discount to less than $17\frac{1}{2}$%; in fact, Hood had taken a profit of about 5% on the £2.12s.6d. which he himself had presumably paid. When Edwards bought direct from the wholesaler, his discount was exactly $17\frac{1}{2}$%.

This example does not merely confirm the accuracy of Johnson's description and our extrapolations from it. It also emphasises that the country bookseller had to apply to the right supplier if he was to

The Provincial Book Trade

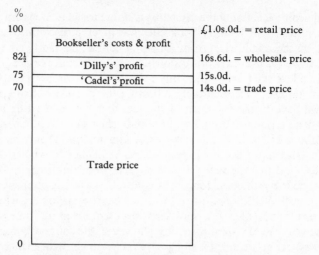

Diagram 1. Costs and profits: Johnson's calculation

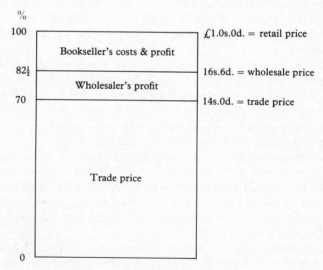

Diagram 2. Costs and profits: through a wholesaler

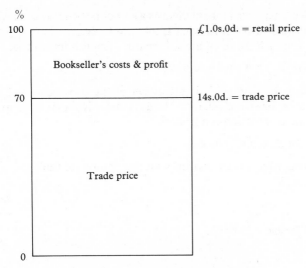

Diagram 3. Costs and profits: direct supply

maximise his discount and hence his profit. For convenience, we will follow Johnson in referring to this supplier as the wholesaler, and we shall now consider his role, since it was clearly so vital to the country bookseller.

WHOLESALERS AND DISTRIBUTORS

Who were the wholesalers? How can we identify them? More importantly, how did the country bookseller know who was wholesaling a particular book? It will be recalled that Clavell had asked users of the *Term Catalogues* 'to say who they are, or were Printed for, that when such Orders reach *London* they might be got with the more ease'. The phrase 'Printed for' is the clue, suggesting that it is in the imprint that we should look for information about wholesaling.

Imprints can be puzzling. We know that they tell us a good deal about the ownership of copyrights, and that the order of names was a careful reflection of the relative seniority of the shareholders.[54] We also know that they contain information about marketing arrangements, although work on this aspect of the study of imprints has concentrated on the pamphlet publishers who hovered on the edge of the law.[55] The evidential value of imprints for our purposes can best be understood if we look on them as a sort of book-trade code which, once cracked, can tell us what it told the trade.

The fullest form of eighteenth-century English imprint is:

Printed by X, for Y, and sold by Z.

Here X is the printer, Y is the owner of the copyright, and Z the distributor or wholesaler.[56] More commonly, the imprint was abbreviated, omitting the printer:

Printed for Y, and sold by Z.

If the copyright owner was his own distributor we find:

Printed for Y.

or:

Printed for and sold by Y.

or:

Printed and sold by Y.

The variations all retain the essential information: the name of the distributor. In other words, the imprint, unless deliberately deceptive, is always concerned with marketing.

We can now take a few examples of London books which will illustrate some details and variations of these practices. A typical example of a single bookseller acting as his own distributor is this imprint from a book published by John Nourse:[57]

London, Printed for J. Nourse at the Lamb opposite Katherine-Street in the Strand. MDCCLX.

Nourse gives his address; this is not merely for advertising purposes, but also so that orders can be properly directed, for it will be recalled that in advertisements and lists of books in print the imprint, or at least names and abbreviated addresses, are reproduced from the forms used in the book.

A slightly more complicated example is an edition of Ossian published in 1790:

London: Printed for A. Strahan; and T. Cadell, In The Strand. MDCCXC.

If imprints were indeed a code we have to assume that all distinctions are significant. Two questions therefore arise here. Why is there a semi-colon after Strahan's name? And why is Cadell's address given when Strahan's is not? Cadell went into partnership with the elder Strahan in 1780, and with the younger after his father's death in 1785, but they retained separate premises.[58] Both owned shares in the Ossian copyright; Strahan had inherited that bought by his father in 1773, and Cadell had bought a share in 1784.[59] Yet the imprint does imply a distinction between them. This distinction is that Cadell was handling the distribution from his shop in The Strand, and that it was thither, and not to one of Strahan's several addresses, that the trade were to apply for their copies. The semi-colon and the address indicate that this was so.

The copyright owner, or a sharer, was not always the distributor, as can be seen from this example:[60]

London: Printed for T. Pitcher, No. 44 Barbican; Also sold by C. Dilly, Poultry; T. Parsons, Paternoster-Row; and T. Mathews, Strand. M. DCC. XC.

Pitcher was the copyright owner; the book was printed 'for' him, and he was the man whose capital was at risk. He also, apparently, acted as his own distributor, but there were other distributors, with no shares in the copyright, who also acted as distributors, like 'Cadel' in Johnson's example. Their profits came from the wholesaler's mark-up.

It was not, however, always the case that all the wholesale distributors were in London:[61]

London: Printed and Sold by R. Hindmarsh, No. 32, Clerkenwell-Close. Sold also by J. Buckland, Pater-noster-Row; J. Denis, New Bridge-Street, Fleet-Street; W. Brown, Corner of Essex-Street, Strand; J. Cuthell, Middle-Row, Holborn; I. Clarke and J. Haslingden, Manchester; T. Mills, Bristol; and may be had by giving Orders to any of the Booksellers in Town and Country. M. DCC. LXXX. VII.

Robert Hindmarsh was the copyright owner, or his agent. There are also four other London wholesalers or distributors: Buckland, Denis, Brown, and Cuthell. The imprint, however, equates these four with Isaac Clarke and John Haslingden in Manchester, and Thomas Mills in Bristol. They were, it seems, performing the same function in their respective cities and regions as were the four London booksellers in town.

For some books, regional distributors were more than a luxury:[62]

London: Printed for E. and C. Dilly, in the Poultry; and Sold by Messrs Goadby in Sherborne, Thorn in Exeter, Haydon in Plimouth, Tozer in Modbury, Painter in Truro, Allison in Falmouth. MDCCLXX.

Thomas Vivian, the author, was a Cornishman, born in Truro; he was Vicar of Cornwood, Devon, for nearly fifty years, and was also well known as a writer.[63] This combination led to his book being published in London and thus being able to take advantage of the national distribution system, while simultaneous provision was made to ensure ease of supply in the counties where the book was likely to be in greatest demand.

The practice of using local booksellers as wholesalers in towns or areas where the book had a special market was common, but one more example, Shaw's *Dictionary*, must suffice:[64]

London: Printed for the Author, by W. and A. Strahan; And sold by J. Murray, Fleet-street; P. Elmsly, Strand; C. Elliott, J. Balfour, and R. Jamieson, Edinburgh; D. Prince, Oxford; Messrs. Merril, Cambridge; Wilson, Dublin; and Pissot, at Paris. MDCCLXXX.

Provision had been made for the distribution of this great and pioneering work of scholarship not only in London, but also in Scotland and Ireland, in the two English universities, and on the continent. Shaw's book was not a best-seller, but the country and foreign booksellers stood to gain if they distributed more copies as wholesalers than they would have sold as retailers. The selection and use of country distributors will be discussed later (pp. 64–67).

TRANSPORT

Before turning to the question of regional and local distribution, we must consider how the books actually reached the provincial booksellers. Speed was not usually important in the distribution of books and, since postage was expensive, cheaper forms of transport were sought. At the beginning of the century this still meant pack-horses in many parts of the country, including virtually the whole of the north of England.[65] The gradual improvement of the roads, however, made wheeled transport possible almost everywhere, and by the end of the century the carrier's waggon had replaced the train of pack-horses as the most familiar sight on the road. The network of carriers was a wide one, radiating not only from London but also from the major provincial towns. In 1794, for example, 202 waggons left Bristol each week, not only for the surrounding area and the west of England, but also for places as far away as Leicester, Nottingham, York, Lincoln, Cambridge, Liverpool, and Birmingham, as well as London, and most of these had onward connections to yet more distant places.[66] The carriers were slow, but they were cheap, and were, as we know from advertisements and from occasional accounts of accidents,[67] used for the transport of books. Even on the turnpikes, the cost of carriage rarely exceeded 1d. per hundredweight per mile.[68]

The carriers did not, however, provide the only means of road transport for books; they were not always very reliable. When Combe, in Leicester, ordered books worth £50 from John Nichols in 1812, he asked for them to be sent down by waggon, with the significant addendum that they should be *'well-packed'*.[69] When speed was important, the coaches were used; Joseph Pote of Eton probably had customers waiting when, on 1 June 1749, he asked John Nourse to send him six books *'per* Windsor Coach on Saturday morn[g]'.[70] There is no doubt of William Harrod's urgency when he wrote to Nichols in 1810 for a copy of one part of Nichols's own *History and antiquities of the county of Leicester*, published in eight parts, each of them a massive folio volume, between 1795 and 1815 (p. 54 above): 'You will therefore be pleased to forward me a Copy immediately, by the Hope Coach, Angel Inn, Angel Street.'[71]

For bulk carriage, when speed was unimportant, water transport was often the preferred method. When Thomas Cadell received George Roots' *The charters of the town of Kingston upon Thames* from the printers in 1797, he wrote to Roots to ask him to arrange for the transport of his own hundred copies to Kingston. He recommended water carriage; even though a coach would be safer, 'from the Size of the Parcel road carriage would be attended with a greater Degree of Expence than . . . Water'.[72] In this instance, the River Thames was the waterway, but elsewhere in the country the canals would have been used; Richard Cruttwell, a Bath bookseller, thought it worth his while to invest in a canal which would improve communications between London and the west.[73] There were, as Cadell implied, dangers inherent in the use of the waterways. Bishop Tanner of St Asaph moved his books from Norwich to Oxford by water in 1731 with disastrous consequences; some fell into the river and were there for twenty hours, a fate from which some of them have never recovered.[74]

The sea was still an important means of communication between northern and southern Britain throughout the century. When, in 1768, Kincaid and Bell of Edinburgh ordered a long list of books from a catalogue issued by Todd and Sotheran in York, they instructed the vendors to 'be so good as to send them to your next Sea Port Town, which we believe is Hull for Leith by the very first Ship'.[75] Similarly, when the Edinburgh firm was in financial difficulties in 1771, and demanded the return of books sent on a sale-or-return basis to William Charnley in Newcastle, they asked that the parcels be sent by sea to Leith, although in 1767, when sending a much smaller quantity of books to Newcastle, they had used a carrier to take them south.[76]

The slower forms of transport – waggon, canal barge, and coastal vessel – were normally used for the carriage of books, and the coaches were used only when speed was essential; the Post Office does not figure at all in the distribution of books, its sphere of activity being confined to the newspapers and perhaps some magazines and part-books. When books eventually reached the country booksellers they were either displayed in the shop as stock, or kept for or sent to a customer who had placed an order; for delivery the local carrier or the newsman was used, as envisaged in the advertisements.

The purchaser could choose his own form of transport since it was he who paid for it. It will be recalled that Edwards complained that his profit was damaged when he was given less than the 17½% discount because he had to bear the lower discount as well as the cost of carriage (p. 57, above). The implication is that transport was regarded as one of the bookseller's costs, but that it was not normally passed on to the customer.

LOCAL DISTRIBUTION

In theory, any bookseller who could establish the soundness of his credit could order books on trade terms from the wholesaler. Indeed, imprints, advertisements, prospectuses, and lists of books in print all emphasise that customers could give their orders to any bookseller in London or the provinces. Many smaller booksellers did indeed order single copies from time to time, as we have seen. Others, like Clay, preferred to deal whenever possible with a single bookseller who was, in effect, his London agent.[77] This system worked perfectly well for single-copy orders or small quantities, but a different mechanism was needed by a London bookseller who wanted a new book to achieve deep penetration of the provincial market. It is this mechanism which we shall now examine: how the London trade used the provincial booksellers as a marketing and distribution system.

The evidence of imprints is again a useful introduction to this subject, as we shall begin with the example already quoted of Vivian's

Exposition (p. 61, above). Goadby was the distributor of the book in the west of England where the author's local connections made it of special interest. He was not the only bookseller in the west country, but he was by far the best-known, and also, because of his newspaper, had the most wide-ranging contacts. The agency system of the provincial newspapers (pp. 23–25, above) made the newspaper owners into ideal local and regional distributors. They knew their regional book trades intimately; they had agents and newsmen who could advertise the book, take orders and payments for it, and deliver or sell the book themselves. They represented, in fact, a ready-made system of deep market penetration. This gave the newspapers a key role in the provincial trade. They were, for the most part, printed in regional capitals with easy communication with London; their owners had good credit, as well as good connections; and their role as distributors merely increased their existing dominance of the trade in their region.

This crucial link between the provincial newspapers and book distribution was often explicit. In 1761, an advertisement appeared in *The Northampton Mercury* which listed a considerable number of new books. The whole display is headed by this notice:[78]

The following Books, &c. may be had of the Printer hereof [Cluer Dicey], and of the Men who carry this News: Also of the following Booksellers, viz, J. Ellington in Huntingdon, Godmanchester, and St. Neot's, and his Newsmen who distribute this Paper in those Parts; J. Clay, in Daventry, and at his Shops in Rugby and Lutterworth; R. Willcox, in Towcester; B. Seeley, in Buckingham; J. Ratten, in Market Harborough and Kettering; and Ratten and Parker in Coventry.

Here the local order and distribution system is clear. Dicey's newsmen, Ellington's newsmen in Huntingdonshire, and the agents will all take orders and sell the books. When the orders reached the newspaper owner, he transmitted them to London, as Harvey Berrow of Worcester had explained in the previous year:[79]

All Sorts of Books, Pamphlets, Acts of Parliament, The several Magazines, And All Other Periodical Publications, Are continued to be sold by H. Berrow, Goose Lane, Worcester; Who procures them from London as soon as possible after they are bespoke, which is the usual Method with Country Booksellers, whose Orders are supply'd Weekly from thence.

Books like Vivian's which had a particular local interest could take advantage of the same system, and the local distributor could take an extra share in the profits in return for the wider distribution which he was able to provide. He was, as Johnson pointed out, essentially a

65

warehouser, and incurred no real risks. Another example of the same practice, from 1793, is James Wood's *Thoughts on the effects of the application and abstraction of stimuli on the human body*:

London: Printed for J. Murray, Fleet-Street; and W. Creech, Edinburgh: And sold by W. Charnley, R. Fisher, and S. Hodgson, Newcastle; W. Phorson, Berwick; J. Graham, Sunderland; R. Christopher, Stockton; and L. Pennington, Durham.

Wood was a member of the Royal Medical Society of Edinburgh, and a physician at the Newcastle Dispensary; hence the listing of seven booksellers in the north-east.

Not all imprints have provincial names; indeed, in books of general interest they are uncommon save in the rare cases where there was a provincial shareholder in the copyright. From the middle of the century onwards, however, such phrases as 'sold by all the booksellers in town and country' became more common, and indicated to the trade that the book was generally available through the usual channels in the regional centres. Occasionally, this bald statement is padded out by listing some of the leading provincial booksellers in major towns, to give wide regional coverage:[80]

London; Printed for the Author, and (by his Appointment) sold by J. Coote, in Pater-Noster-Row, London; Mr. Fletcher, in Oxford; Mr. Merril, at Cambridge; Mr. Leake, at Bath; Mr. Etherington and Hinxman at York; Mr. Fleming, at Edinburgh; Mr. Wilson, in Dublin; and all other Booksellers in Great Britain and Ireland.

Even when no provincial distributors are named, the newspaper owners were still a key element in distribution. Smollett's edition of Voltaire (1761) was printed for Newbery, Baldwin, Crowder, Coote, Johnstone, and Kearsley in London, 'And Sold by all Booksellers in Great Britain and Ireland'. It appears in the advertisement in *The Northampton Mercury*, headed by the notice quoted on p. 65. In *The York Courant* (1850 (7 Apr. 1761)) the advertisement gives the imprint, adding 'Sold by C. Etherington, in Coney-Street, and W. Tesseyman, in the Minster-Yard, York'. In his *Worcester Journal*, Berrow also reproduced the imprint, with this supplement:

Particularly by H. Berrow, at the Printing Office in Goose Lane, Worcester; and by the several Booksellers in Worcester, Shrewsbury, Bridgnorth, Bewdley, Kidderminster, Stowerbridge, Gloucester, Tewkesbury, Hereford, Ludlow, Coventry, Lichfield, Stafford, Warwick, Stratford-upon-Avon, Leominster, and Evesham. Of whom Proposals may be had.

The 'several Booksellers' were Berrow's newsagents, and are often listed by name in his book advertisements. By using them, through Berrow, the London booksellers could reach a much wider market than they could otherwise have done.

By the 1780s the system was sufficiently complex to call for a printed guide to assist the increasing number of London booksellers seeking a country market for their publications, a number further increased by the greater freedom to reprint older texts after the House of Lords' decision of 1774. Such a guide was provided in 1785 by John Pendred, an otherwise insignificant member of the London trade, in his *Vade Mecum*.[81] Pendred was deliberately selective in both his London and country lists. The country list is, in effect, of the principal booksellers who were able to handle local distribution, and in this light the 'omissions' noted by Pollard,[82] although a few may be accidental errors, are to be seen as being, for the most part, qualitative judgements. The list of country newspapers[83] is the key to understanding Pendred. He gives forty-nine titles in thirty-four towns and cities; all but five of the newspaper printers also appear in the general list of the country trade,[84] and three of them are in cities where there was more than one newspaper.[85]

Pendred's *Vade Mecum* helped the London trade in three ways. First, it gave them easy access to information about advertising in the provinces, should they require it for books of special local interest. Each entry for a country newspaper includes a note of the paper's London agent, most of them coffee-house keepers, who took in advertisements. Some papers had several agents; all had at least one. Secondly, Pendred told the London trade who were the owners of the provincial newspapers; they knew that each owner had his network of agents and newsmen whom they could exploit to advertise and distribute their books. Thirdly, the list of booksellers filled in the gaps for the lesser towns which had no newspaper of their own. The country sections of *Vade Mecum* are in fact a guide to how to use the country trade. All of those whose names we have noted in advertisements, prospectuses, and imprints are to be found there. The country booksellers not listed by Pendred are the lesser men, the newsagents and others who worked through booksellers in their regional centres. They might order books, but they could not assist in the distribution of large quantities.

Our picture of the distribution system is now complete and we can now understand the extent of the interdependence of the London and country trades, and their reluctance to embark on serious quarrels. From the London point of view, the system consisted of advertising media which informed both the trade and its customers of what books were, or soon would be, available; a wholesaling system which controlled discounts; and a distribution system which enabled them to reach everywhere served by a provincial newspaper, which, by the middle of the century, meant virtually the whole of England. It gave them access to a national market which could sustain and support book production on an economic scale. From a provincial viewpoint it provided stock in a manner which was efficient enough to encourage customers to buy from their local bookseller rather than directly from London, and did so in a way which provided reasonable profits when the unwritten rules, coded in imprints, were properly followed. The Londoners were the producers; the country booksellers were the retailers. So long as that balance was maintained harmony and profit went hand in hand.

CHAPTER 5

The Bookselling Business

A Youth designed for a Bookseller, ought to have a Genius for Letters, a general Knowledge of Books and Sciences, a clear Head, and a solid discerning Judgment: He ought to have a Taste for the Languages, and a good Memory to acquire them. His Education ought to be as liberal as if he was designed for any of the learned Sciences; and his Knowledge of Men and Things as extensive as either the Divine, Lawyer, or Physician. A mere Title-Monger can never make any thing but a Bungler, is liable every Day to be imposed upon, runs out his Stock upon Trifles, and loads the Public with the Rubbish of the Press.[1]

The ideal bookseller portrayed by Campbell was not entirely unknown in the eighteenth century, even in the provinces, but he was uncommon. At the other extreme, as late as 1787 Lackington claimed to have found that, in practice, there was nothing but 'Trifles' and the 'rubbish of the Press':[2]

It is true, at York and Leeds there were a few (and but very few) good books; but in all the other towns between London and Edinburgh nothing but trash was to be found.

Lackington was trying to prove that he had transformed English bookselling, while Campbell, as is clear from his Preface, was pursuing a vendetta against the trade. Yet both statements have a germ of truth in them. It was not easy to keep a good bookshop successfully in a country town; Thomas Miller discovered at Bungay, Suffolk between 1755 and 1804, that a good stock was not in itself a guarantee of success in business.[3]

In this chapter, we shall consider the bookseller's business in some detail. So far we have looked at how the country trade obtained books, the market which they served, and their legal and economic relationship with the London producers. Now we enter the country bookshop itself. What sort of shop was it? What stock was to be found on the shelves? How profitable was the trade? And who were the men who followed it?

The Provincial Book Trade

There is no adequate contemporary representation of the interior of an ordinary English bookshop of the eighteenth century. The familiar picture of Lackington's Temple of the Muses in Finsbury Square, London, is hardly typical, for it fulfilled its owner's intention that it should be the largest bookshop in England.[4] Other pictures are either of London bookshops or of circulating libraries. The portrait of Susanna Oakes of Ashbourne, Derbyshire, shows her in her circulating library, but there is no detail beyond a few shelves of books.[5] We must rely largely on documentary sources to reconstruct the appearance and contents of the shop.

The size and value of premises used as bookshops varied enormously. In 1794, James Liddell of Bodmin, Cornwall, insured his house, shop, and offices, all 'under one roof', for a mere £100.[6] The combination of shop and house in a single building was still common at the end of the century among the smaller booksellers. In the following year, John Bredon of Tenterden, Kent, had a combined house and shop worth £200;[7] Peter Walker of Cockermouth, Cumberland, had similar premises worth £150.[8] The larger firms naturally had more elaborate establishments. John Merrill the younger of Cambridge had a 'workshop and warehouse adjoining' his dwelling house, and another warehouse in St Michael's parish;[9] on an even larger scale, William Clachar of Chelmsford, Essex, had his stock divided between his house, two warehouses, two or possibly three printing offices, and assorted outbuildings.[10]

The exterior of a shop in Brighton, Sussex, is fairly clearly portrayed in the engraving on the title-page of A. Crawford's *Description of Brighthelmstone* published in 1788 (Plate 1). Crawford was both author and publisher, and, as the illustration makes very clear, the owner of a circulating library. He was also, however, a bookseller, stationer, and bookbinder, as can be seen from the signs along the edge of the balcony. From this picture it would seem that a few tables of books were displayed outdoors, beneath the balcony. The entrance was presumably at the side, or facing the sea on the other side of the building. The whole building as shown here looks very much like a house which had been converted into a combined house and shop.

The premises of the Marine Library a few miles down the coast at Hastings were apparently very similar. The picture in Plate 2 was published in 1797 in *The Hastings Guide*, but the building itself seems

70

and

THE ADJACENT COUNTRY;

or

The New Guide for Ladies and Gentlemen
using that Place of Health and Amusement .

CRAWFORD's
CIRCULATING LIBRARY

(POST OFFICE) BOOKSELLER STATIONER & BOOKBINDER (POST OFFICE)

E.Paine delin.

Of purest Air and healing Waves we tell,
Where welcome Maid Hygiæa loves to dwell .

BRIGHTHELMSTONE :
Printed for A. CRAWFORD .

Plate 1. Crawford's circulating library, Brighton, c.1788

71

to date from the early 1790s in this form. Again it looks like a converted house, and we know something of the internal arrangements: 'Over the Library is a very good Billiard Room, from which there is a fine view of the sea. Near the Library is the Marine Cottage, a very desirable Lodging House.'[11] These two libraries give us some idea of the appearance of a bookshop, but they were different from them in being designed to attract the fashionable clientele of a seaside resort. The urban bookshops were less likely to be in separate buildings; it is clear from insurance policies that many were in rows of tenements.

For the internal fittings of a small bookshop we can turn to the inventory of Ellen Feepound's shop in Stafford, compiled when she went bankrupt in 1776:[12]

Two old Chairs
A Looking Glass
A Nest of Drawers
Three Glass Cases for Books and three Drawers under one of them
A large Counter
A Coffer
Eight Dale [Deal?] Boxes
Several Shelves
and a Small pair of Scales and Brass weights viz.ᵗ a 2^{lb}, 1^{lb}, $\frac{1}{2}^{lb}$, 4^{oz}, 2^{oz}, 1^{oz}, $\frac{1}{2}^{oz}$, $\frac{1}{4}^{oz}$, and a Cloth Yard.

This humble establishment was very different from the seaside circulating libraries. There was limited shelf space, and a good deal of the stock other than books must have been out of sight in drawers and boxes, or displayed on the counter or in the windows. The scales and yardstick point to the sale of goods other than books and paper. Nothing which needed weighing is listed in the inventory; nor indeed is any haberdashery, but the yardstick might have been used for measuring wallpaper. We cannot know whether Miss Feepound's fixtures and equipment were typical, but we may take it that her shop was not unique among the small country bookshops.

STOCK: BOOKS

The value, size, and contents of the stock varied from shop to shop, but it is possible to assemble a general picture from various sources. One objective measurement of value, and hence to some extent of

Plate 2. The Marine Library, Hastings, c.1792

size, is to be found in insurance valuations.[13] There is great variation, as might be expected: Thomas Magrie of Bridport, Dorset, had stock worth £35,[14] while William Clachar insured his for £2,300.[15] Nearly half of the booksellers who had policies with the Sun in the 1790s, however, insured their stock for between £100 and £500,[16] and only a handful had stock valued at more than £1,000.[17] Comparisons with other trades are not easy to make. Campbell put bookselling among the more expensive trades in which to set up business, but he was writing of the London trade and had in mind copy-owning rather than stockholding booksellers.[18] In 1837, about £500 was regarded as a 'fair capital' to establish a firm, about the same as that required for a butcher, haberdasher, or ironmonger.[19] In short, our average country bookseller with less than £500 invested in his stock was working at about the same level as other specialist country shopkeepers.

For the contents of the stock we can rely on a number of sources: contemporary commentators, inventories, and advertisements and catalogues. Together they provide a reasonable picture of the contents of a country bookshop throughout the century.

At the beginning of the century, Michael Johnson's stock in Lichfield was agreed to be excellent. It was in his shop that his son read 'all ancient writers, all manly: though but little Greek' before going up to Oxford.[20] According to George Plaxton, Chaplain to Lord Gower and one of Johnson's regular customers, 'Johnson . . . propagates learning all over the diocese',[21] and, in a letter to Plaxton, Johnson used a phrase which suggests that he regularly bought new books for his stock.[22] Johnson was a good bookseller of the generation before the newspapers, following in the footsteps of men like Awdeley (p. 1, above). Classics and divinity, however, were not the bulk of the trade. In Chester at the end of the seventeenth century, John Minshull calculated that he had sold 144 copies of *A week's preparation for the Lord's Supper*, and 748 copies of nine school books. This was more typical of a bookseller's trade at that time.[23]

In the middle years of the century there is a degree of uniformity in booksellers' advertisements which suggests a certain standardisation of stocks. John Hogben's handbill (p. 25, above) begins:

All Sorts of Bibles, and Common Prayers, Books of Divinity, History, and all other Books, both Ancient and Modern.

Thomas Payne of Wrexham, at about the same time, 'Sells Books in all Faculties, Bibles, Common Prayer Books'.[24] In 1730, Thomas Hammond of York (Plate 3) sold 'Bibles, Prayer-Books, School-Books, Histories, Law, Physick-Books, and others of various Sorts. Newest Pamphlets'. At an auction held in Great Yarmouth by the Norwich bookseller Henry Crossgrove in 1720, well over half the books were theological.[25] The overwhelming impression is that stocks were dominated by theology, and that Bibles and Prayer Books were the one class of literature which could be guaranteed a place on the shelves of any country bookshop.

Religion, however, was not the only subject to be found in some shops. Both Luke Hansard and William Hutton paid tribute to booksellers in the middle of the century. Hansard considered Berry and Booth of Norwich to be 'men with learning',[26] a claim sustained by the issue of a substantial catalogue in 1773.[27] When Hutton moved to Birmingham in 1750 he 'found three eminent booksellers for mental improvement, *Aris*, *Warren*, and *Wollaston*'.[28] He contrasted this with his experience in Southwell, Nottinghamshire, a 'town as despicable as the road to it', where in the previous year he had unsuccessfully established a bookshop and 'in one day became the most eminent bookseller in the place'.[29] The regional capitals were able to sustain some good, well-stocked bookshops by the middle of the eighteenth century; smaller towns could not generally do so.

For a more specific study of a bookseller's stock, we can turn to an advertisement issued by Samuel Mountfort of Worcester in 1760 (Plate 4).[30] Mountfort had been in business in Worcester since the 1720s, and seems to have been the town's leading bookseller for the next twenty or twenty-five years.[31] The stock partly reflects the function of the city as a regional capital. Worcester was a cathedral city, a county town, and, above all, a market town; its hinterland had been largely agricultural since the decline of its cloth trade in the seventeenth century, and the northern parts of the county, which were becoming industrialised, looked towards Birmingham rather than Worcester as their economic focus.[32]

No fewer than twelve of the books are legal texts or treatises, and there are also three transcripts of trials. Some of the legal works relate to the interests and needs of landowners,[33] Justices of the Peace and other local functionaries,[34] and tradesmen.[35] There are, however, some more general works, including Hawkins's edition of *The statutes at large*, and Blackstone's books on charters, collateral consanguinity, and fee simple, and his *Analysis of the law*. The second largest category of non-fiction was of works on religion. We might expect this in a

BIbles, Prayer-Books, School-Books, Histories, Law, Phyfick-Books, and others of various Sorts. Neweft Pamphlets, Paper-Books, Pocket-Books of any Size, Rul'd or Unrul'd, Books with Ivory Leafs, Velum-Leafs, Slate-Leafs, Writing-Paper of various Prices, Paper Frofted and Plain Colours, Im-koft and Marble-Paper, Cap-Paper, Yard-Papers for hanging Rooms, &c. Gilt and Mourning Letter-Papers, Letter-Cafes, Writing-Slates, Pencils that draws black and red ; Camel-hair-Pencils, Sealing-Wax, Wafers, Spectacles, fineft white Glafs, Glafs Grafs-green in Silver Frames, and Tortoife-Shell, other fine and ordinary Sorts, with Cafes, Maps and Landskips, Prof-pects for Stair-Cafes, other Copper-Plates and Metzo-Tinto Prints of various Sorts, Lottery-Pictures and other ordinary Sorts; Almanacks, Letter-Files, Ink-Powder, Harbin's Shining Japan-Ink, Cake-Ink, Indian-Ink, Writing-Parchment, black Lead, fine Pounce, Pumice Stone, Affidue or Horfe-Gold, Hobby-Horfe Bells, Prospect Glaffes with Microfcopes and without, Telefcopes, burning and reading Glaffes in Tortoife-Shell and other plain Sorts. Ink Glaffes alfo fet in Brafs of divers Sorts, Wainfcot and Pewter-Standifhes, Ring-Dials, Sand and Wafer-Boxes, Shagreen Ink-Cafes for the Pocket, Prickers for Parchment, Ivory Knives for Cutting and Folding Paper, Black Glittering Sand, &c.

Alfo Mathematical Books and Inftruments of various Sorts for Surveying, Navigation, Excife, &c. and fine Vellum for drawing Maps of Eftates, &c. for Surveyors, Leaf Gold and Silver.

By THOMAS HAMMOND, Jun. *Bookfeller in* York.

He will give Ready Money for any Library or Parcel of Books.

Where may be had Dr. *Anderfon*'s Scots Pills, 12 *d. per* Box. *Squire*'s Grand Elixir, or the Great Reftorative of the World, at 15 *d.* and 2 *s.* 6 *d.* the Bottle. *Stoughton*'s Great Cordial Elixir for the Stomach, 1 *s. per* Bottle. *Tipping*'s pleafant Liquor excellent againft the Stone and Gravel, Cholick, Gout, Rheumatifm, 3 *s.* 6 *d. per* Bottle. *Hungary* Water. Dr. *Peter*'s Pills, at 12 *d. per* Box. .... Cordial Tincture at 2 *s.* 6 *d. per* Bottle. Spirits of Scurvy-Grafs, golden and plain, 12 *d.* each. Dr. *Eaton*'s Balfamick Styptick, at 2 *s.* 6 *d. per* Bottle. Dr. *Bateman*'s Pectoral Drops, at 12 *d. per* Bottle. Balfam of *Chili* 18 *d. per* Bottle.

Plate 3. Thomas Hammond's advertisement, 1730

New BOOKS, printed this Season,

TO BE HAD OF

SAMUEL MOUNTFORT,

Bookseller and Stationer,

Near the *Guild-Hall*, in *High-Street*, WORCESTER.

STATUTES, Vol. 7th, 8th, 9th, to compleat Hawkins's Edition, formerly publish'd, Folio.
Montaigne's Works, 3 Vols. Octavo.
Morris's Plan for arranging and ballancing Accounts of Landed Estates, Folio.
Blackstone's Great Charter and Charter of the Forest.
Complete System of Family Book-keeping, by Mrs. Walker
Lindsay's Voyage to Africa, with an Account of the Taking of Goree, Quarto.
Osmer on the Diseases and Lameness of Horses.
Bartlet's Farriery.
Solicitor's Guide, and Tradesman's Instructor, concerning Bankrupts.

OCTAVO.

Stanhope's Epistles and Gospels, 4 Vols new.
Ditto, *second-hand, very fair*.
Bentivoglio's Letters.
Lond. and Country Brewer.
British Housewife, 2 Vols.
Kirkpatrick on Inoculation.
Haller's Medical, Chirurgical and Anatomical Cases.
Institutes of Experimental Chemistry, 2 Vols.
Mackenzie on Health.
Pott of Wounds and Contusions of the Head, &c.
Sydenham's Treatise on Fevers
Brookes's Introduction to Physick.
Hill's Treat. on Fruit Trees
Huxham on Air.
Servants' Directory.
Blackstone's Analysis of the Law.
Do. of Descents in Fee Simple
Treatise on Rents.
——— on Court of Exchequer, by a late Ld Baron
New Compleat Parish Officer
Life of Ld. Clarendon, 3 V.
Moral and Political Dialogues.
Smith's Moral Sentiments.
Present State of Europe.

Montague on the Rise and Fall of antient Republicks
Remarks on the Tenets and Principles of Quakers.
Life of King David, 2 Vols.
Royal Authors, 2 Vols.
Farrier's Directory.
Reeves's Farriery.
List of the Army.
Demonstrations on Religion and Virtue.
Advice from a Bishop to a young Clergyman.
Life of General Wolfe.
Political and Satyrical Hist of the Years 1756, 1757
Musical Dictionary.
Knapp on the Psalms.
Playford on the Psalms.
Essay on Collateral Consanguinity.
Hillary on Properties of Fire
Considerations on the Laws of the Poor.
——— on the Question, *Whether Tenants by Copy of Court Roll are Free holders*
Life and Trial of Eug. Aram
——— of Stevenson.
——— of Aylisse.

TWELVES.

Beauties of Shakespear, 2 V.
Life and Opinions of Tristram Shandy, 2 Vols.
Poems on Subjects chiefly devotional, 2 Vols.
The Mother, or Happy Distress, 2 Vols.
Nuptial Dialogues, 2 Vols.
Love Letters between a Nobleman and his Sister, 2 V.
Warning-Piece against Murder.
Forms of Devotion for Families.
Short View of Irish Peerage.

British Legacy, or Fountain of Knowledge.
Housekeeper's Pocket Book.
News Readers Pocket Book, or Military Dictionary.
History of Masonry.
Shepperd's Vulg. Arithmetic
How's Meditations.
Indiana, a modern Novel.
Every Farmer his own Farrier.
Hist of the Marquess de Cressy.
Hoyle's Games compleat.
World display'd, No 1, 2, 3

Newbery's History and Constitution of England;
And all his small entertaining
STORY and HISTORY-BOOKS for CHILDREN.

NEW PLAYS.

Desert Island.
High Life below Stairs.
Cleone.
The Rout.
Rival Theatres.
Insolvent, or Filial Piety.

The Guardian.
Cymbeline, *alter'd*.
Orphan of China.
Titus Vespasian.
Caractacus
Oroonoko, *alter'd*.

And most of the best Old PLAYS, single.

*** Doddridge's Family Expositor—All Weekly and Monthly Publications—And most of the Political Pamphlets published since the Beginning of the present War.

Fine PRINTS of the
Prince of Wales, Prince Edward, Prince Ferdinand,
And several others of eminent Persons, publish'd last Year.

☞ ON SALE, *at the same Shop*,

Several Parcels of BOOKS, purchas'd this Winter, in very good Condition.—Chambers's Dictionary, *second-hand*, to be sold. —— A small Deal Book-Case to be sold cheap.

N. B. Mitchell's Map of America, in Eight Sheets—— Four-Sheet Map of Germany, on Canvas, with Rollers, colour'd—Ditto, North America, all lately publish'd.

†*† Fine Scotch Inkhorns, just imported.

The TENTHS of the CLERGY are return'd, as usual, to the End of April next.

Plate 4. Samuel Mountfort's advertisement, 1760

cathedral city, but in fact some of Mountfort's theological stock was of works for the pious laity: George Stanhope's paraphrases, *Forms of devotion for the use of pious families* (1758), and the much-reprinted translation of the Psalms by John Playford. There are some new books which would have been of interest to the clergy, including, for example, the anonymous *Two discourses or demonstrations on religion and virtue*. One work which was no doubt in considerable local demand was *Moral and political dialogues* (1759), published anonymously, but known to have been written by Richard Hurd, the Archdeacon of Worcester.[36]

Historical and geographical works constituted another large category, and included a very substantial and expensive book by John Lindsay, *A voyage to the coast of Africa* (1759). Perhaps we should also include here Horace Walpole's *Catalogue of the royal and noble authors of Great Britain* (2 vols., 1759). The biography of Wolfe presumably sold well only six months after the fall of Québec and the General's death. Four other items also recall Britain's involvement in a worldwide war: a history of the years 1756 and 1757; *The news-reader's pocket-book, or military dictionary*, published by Newbery and Carnan in 1759; the latest *Army list*; and 'most of the Political Pamphlets published since the Beginning of the Present War'. If this latter claim was true, Mountfort must indeed have had a substantial stock. His customers, if we may judge from this advertisement, shared with the members of the book clubs and proprietary libraries a taste for history, geography, and current affairs.

A book which probably sold well was James MacKenzie's *History of health, and the art of preserving it*, a popular treatise on diet and the digestive system; it was first published in 1758, and had reached its third edition by 1760. There was a special reason for Mountfort to stock it, for the author had been a physician at the Worcester Royal Infirmary from 1745, when it opened, until 1751. The book was dedicated to Isaac Maddox, Bishop of Worcester, who was effectively the founder of the Infirmary.[37] Mountfort stocked a number of other scientific and medical books; like the law books, they are a mixture of the technical and the popular.

Worcester's role as a regional capital and market town is very apparent from Mountfort's stock. In addition to the works on land law, there are books on farriery, and one on fruit-growing; the latter was very important in the nearby Vale of Evesham. For the tradesmen there are works on accountancy and mathematics, and for the housewife three titles on domestic economy. Leisure hours could be whiled away with the aid of Edward Hoyle's famous book on card games, in which, among other things, he established the laws of whist; or they could be devoted to lighter fare, including the twelve plays, four novels, and two volumes of verse which Mountfort advertised and which were only a selection from his stock of fiction and *belles-lettres*.

The most striking features of Mountfort's list are its seriousness, and the fact that it consists almost entirely of comparatively newly published books. He was offering a good representative selection of recent books in all fields, and the implication is that in such a town there was a market for them. Similar shops, with minor regional variations in stock according to location and function, were to be found in all the regional capitals.

Ellen Feepound's stock in Stafford some fifteen years later was very different.[38] Theology was prominent, but little of it was contemporary, and indeed the whole stock was distinctly old-fashioned. The bulk of the theological works appear to have come from a library of seventeenth-century books,[39] with a few of the early eighteenth century by such Anglican stalwarts as Bishop Fleetwood. There were some more recent books, including paraphrases of the Psalms, William Darney's *Hymns* (1751), and popular devotional works. The law books were equally out-of-date. The two *Abridgements* were those of Wingate (1655) and Washington (1704), but there were also some of the practical guides for lawyers and laymen which were in Mountfort's shop. Like Mountfort, Miss Feepound also had a substantial stock of medical books, and her school books included Bailey, Willymot, William Walker's *Treatise of English particles* (1663 and later editions), and Edmund Wingate's *Arithmetic made easy* (1650 and later editions), all still in regular use in the schools despite their age.

The stock is much less impressive than Mountfort's. Indeed these are exactly the kind of books which Lackington claimed to have found in the provincial bookshops at about this time: old-fashioned, second-hand, and largely out-of-date, with little attempt to keep a reasonable stock of current literature. Which, if either, was typical? We cannot know, but it may be significant that Mountfort kept his shop for a quarter of a century, while Ellen Feepound went bankrupt. It seems reasonable to conclude that while there were some well-stocked shops, only the prosperous regional centres could support them. Booksellers in smaller and less wealthy places had to manage as best they could, selling their Bibles, school books, and penny histories, for the market was too small to support more than a few stockholding booksellers.

John Nichols, with his vast knowledge of the trade, is perhaps our best guide to the country booksellers in the last third of the century. From him we learn of a number of good booksellers in country towns, although not all of them were financially successful. Miller of Bungay (p. 69, above) failed because his stock was too good for his limited market. John Woodyer of Cambridge came close to Campbell's ideal of the learned bookseller, for he had 'extensive knowledge';[40] he was no businessman, however, and the firm began to fail after the death of his partner John Thurlbourne. Towards the end of the century bookselling became easier with the growth of the market. Even in the cultural desert of the east midlands, Thomas Combe was 'greatly encouraged' at Leicester.[41] Less surprisingly, John Todd, in business at York from 1757 until his death in 1811, had a very good business, and issued a succession of impressive catalogues. Nichols had high praise for him: 'Few Country Booksellers had exerted themselves with greater ardour and perseverance.'[42] There were also the eccentrics. Nichols applied the word to William Harrod, who had shops at Market Harborough, Leicestershire, Stamford, Lincolnshire, and Mansfield, Nottinghamshire,[43] but we might also include William Flackton of Canterbury, who was sixty years in the trade, and, as a devout Anglican, refused to stock 'impious or profligate' books.[44]

Stockholding booksellers did not have an easy time, but they did exist, and a few, who were in the right places, were as successful in business as they were in following Michael Johnson's example as propagators of learning.

STOCK: STATIONERY

The great majority of the booksellers could not survive on bookselling alone. The lesser men, or those in smaller towns, needed other occupations. We have already noted a number of schoolmasters (p. 35, above). We can add many other trades: Robert Williamson of Liverpool was a cotton broker;[45] John Cheney of Banbury was a haberdasher (p. 26, above); John Bagnall of Ipswich was a metalworker;[46] Thomas Dagnall of Aylesbury, like William Jackson in Oxford, was a banker.[47] *The Universal British Directory* lists booksellers who were also linen drapers (William Angel of Chippenham, Wiltshire, and two others), silversmiths (John Russell of Guildford, Surrey, who also sold cutlery),[48] milliners (Mrs Hicks of Oakham, Rutland), and even an undertaker (Isaac James of Bristol). By far the most common occupation other than bookselling, however, was the sale of stationery, the origin and still the mainstay of the country book trade. 'Bookseller and stationer' is a designation found everywhere. Just over half of all the booksellers in *The Universal British Directory* are also described as stationers, but throughout the previous century the sale of stationery in bookshops had been so common that it was scarcely necessary to mention it. It was the usual, indeed probably the invariable, practice for a bookshop to sell paper.

The range of stationery goods sold was very wide. Payne in Wrexham (note 24) sold 'Shop-Books, Pocket-Books, Gilt and Plain Writing Paper, with all other sorts of Stationery'. Sanderson in Durham (p. 34, above) was more specific in 1767:

all Sorts of Stationery Wares, as Writing Paper, Paper Books for Accompts, Ledgers, Journals, Waste Books, Musick Books, Letter Cases, Maps, Landskips, and Mezzotinto Prints, Sealing Wax, Wafers, Slates, Quills, Pens, Pencils; Standishes, Japon Ink, Ink Powder, Indian Ink.

Hammond's list (Plate 3) was even more detailed, and covers a similar range of paper, pens, inks, and miscellaneous materials related to writing. The bookshop was the place to buy everything of this kind, and stationery goods provided an important source of income for the bookseller.

How important it was obviously varied. In the smaller shop stationery was far more significant than books. John Clay sold comparatively few books, and was not well stocked, but he made a good living out of his stationery trade.[49] Clay's accounts reveal that the bulk of his stationery business was the supply of law stationery, for all his large customers were lawyers. He sold them printed forms, blank sheets of paper and vellum for legal documents, and miscellaneous office supplies. He had a considerable range of qualities and sizes of paper in his shop, and restocked at regular intervals. He seems to have had little storage space, and to have relied on stocking little more than the shop itself could accommodate. Overall, however, the goods which Clay sold correspond closely with those advertised by stationers all over the country.

Like the whole book trade, the stationery trade underwent a major change in the 1730s. After relying on imports for centuries, England at last became self-sufficient in paper, except for high-quality writing papers.[50] At the beginning of the century there were just over a hundred mills in England, heavily concentrated in the south and east, and still operating on a very small scale.[51] By the 1740s, however, white paper for both printing and writing was being produced on a considerable scale,[52] and thereafter the English paper industry expanded rapidly. From the time he first went into business for himself in 1742, Clay bought almost all his paper direct from nearby mills in Northamptonshire and Oxfordshire, occasionally supplemented by supplies from more distant mills, and even less often from wholesale stationers.

Paper of all kinds was readily available in booksellers' shops throughout England by the second quarter of the eighteenth century. Towards the end of the century it became even more important that it should be so as an ancillary to industrial developments. The great growth of the trade in cities like Manchester and Liverpool is partly attributable to the development of the commercial market for paper and packaging. The stationery trade became very profitable, and a few large firms began to emerge. William Hutton abandoned bookselling in 1758, because he thought that the stationery trade would be more profitable amid the rapidly expanding commerce of Birmingham; within ten years his real property alone was worth £2,000.[53] He was the first specialist stationer in the town, and as both wholesaler and retailer had a long and profitable career until his stock was destroyed by rioters in 1791.[54]

Hutton was unique in the scale of his success, but he was not the only large stationer in the provinces. Dickinson Boys of Louth, Lincolnshire, succeeded to his uncle's bookselling business there in 1719. Over the next half-century he developed it into a major wholesale stationery firm, probably beginning by exploiting the ease of importing paper through the east coast ports to which he had easy access. He had a wide regional, and even national, business; John Clay was one of his customers.[55] He continued to sell books, but it was as a stationer rather than a bookseller that he made his name and fortune.

Stationery is perhaps less interesting than books, but in economic terms it was far more important to most provincial booksellers. It provided the solid basis for a business, and, for many, the bulk of their income. It was ubiquitous throughout the country book trade, and no image of a provincial bookshop is complete unless it includes a stock of paper and vellum, and the means of writing upon them.

STOCK: OTHER GOODS

The country bookseller sold books, usually obtained from London, and paper, frequently obtained locally, but this did not exhaust the contents of his shop, or the range of services which he offered. Robert Martin of Launceston, Devon, is described only as a stationer in *The Universal British Directory*; he was also a bookseller, but in addition he sold 'Patent Medicines, Music and Musical Instruments, Perfumery, &c.'[56] One Mr Thorner, who had a shop at Bridport, Dorset, in the middle of the century, also sold 'excellent Pills, Worm Cakes, Eye-Water, and a remedy for Warts'. Joseph Harrop of Manchester was described in *The Universal British Directory* as bookseller, stationer, printer, stamp distributor, medicine vendor, and Post Office Keeper.[57]

The recurrent theme here is patent medicine, which had a very special role in the provincial book trade. This is apparent from the newspaper advertisements for various preparations. In 1738, for example, an advertisement for Duffy's Elixir in *The Leeds Mercury* (653 (15 Aug. 1738)) lists nineteen suppliers in eighteen towns in Yorkshire and east Lancashire, the areas covered by the paper at that time. Not all of them can be identified, but, of those who can, seven were certainly booksellers, and others were agents for *The Leeds Mercury* and may be presumed to have been booksellers. Later in the century, the book trade is even more conspicuous. In 1775, all six regional suppliers of Spilsbury's Antiscorbutic Drops listed in an advertisement in *Berrow's Worcester Journal* (4208 (9 Feb. 1775)) were booksellers, and included two other newspaper proprietors (Robert Raikes of *The Gloucester Journal*, and Myles Swinney of *The Birmingham and Stafford Chronicle*) as well as Berrow himself. Five years later, *The Northampton Mercury* (60:43 (3 Jan. 1780)) carried an advertisement for Beaume de Vie, listing twelve local suppliers of whom all but one were certainly in the book trade and were also newsagents. In the same issue, it was announced that another medicine 'may be had of the Newsmen'. Almost all booksellers seem to have sold medicines. Hammond in York listed ten of them in his very comprehensive advertisement in 1730; Sanderson of Durham listed eight, and had 'various other genuine Medicines' in 1767. Clay sold them in all his shops, although the actual number of bottles sold was not great.[58]

The connection between books and medicine was not new; it can be traced back to the late seventeenth century, and by 1700 many country booksellers were retailing Stoughton's Elixir.[59] Although proprietary medicines have a longer history, their highest point of development was reached only when the newspapers provided a national advertising medium from the eighteenth century onwards.[60] In this sense, the history of the medicine trade resembles that of the book trade; a vast potential market in the provinces was opened up by newspaper advertising, and by using those who sold the newspapers as agents. There was also another important parallel between the two trades; both were concerned with a product which could be obtained at trade prices only from a unique central supplier. The patentee, like the publisher, was a monopolist protected by the law.

The book trade's uniquely widespread distribution system, reaching into every town and village in England, was thus of immense potential value to the medicine patentees. Some leading London booksellers became deeply involved in the medicine trade, and further enhanced the links between books and pharmaceuticals. The most famous of these booksellers was John Newbery, the pioneer publisher of children's books, whose fortune was substantially increased by his ownership of Dr James's Fever Powder from 1746 onwards.[61] This preparation was perhaps the most common of all the patent medicines; it is alleged to have killed Goldsmith, caused the insanity of George III, and saved the life of Christopher Smart.[62] Newbery was a brilliant publicist; in his most famous book, Little Goody Two-Shoes benefits from a dose of the medicine which her publisher owned. Newbery was not the only bookseller to own a medicine; the Beaume de Vie advertised in *The Northampton Mercury* in 1780 was owned by Thomas Becket of The Strand, a 'worthy veteran' of the book trade.[63]

The expansion of the distribution system and its links with the only national advertising medium were the crucial factors in the development of an association between the book and medicine trades. Any producer or provider of services who wanted to work on a national scale faced the same problem as the medicine patentees, and some adopted the same solution. In the 1720s, the Sun Fire Office, established in London in 1710 and anxious to attract provincial business, experimented with the appointment of a 'Riding Officer' who travelled the country in search of customers. The arrangement was very unsatisfactory, and the Sun began to look instead for local traders to act as agents.[64] These traders included many shopkeepers, among whom booksellers were prominent. The Sun's earliest provincial agents included Richard Leggassick, a bookseller in Totnes, Devon (1729), Deverall Dagnall of the Aylesbury bookselling family (1739), and Thomas Collis, a bookseller in Kettering, Northamptonshire (1744). Throughout the century, booksellers acted as insurance agents. The list includes George Burbage of Nottingham (1786), William Clachar in Chelmsford (1785), John Price of Leicester (1797), and our old friend John Hogben of Rye, the Sun's first agent in that town in 1755.[65]

Booksellers were not the only insurance agents, but they were by far the largest group of any one trade involved in the agency business. The Sun and, later, other insurance companies were able to exploit the special position of the booksellers with their combination of metropolitan and local contacts. The agents included several newspaper proprietors, who could make use of their own networks of newsagents and newsmen, and of their immediate access to advertising and sales outlets. Burbage owned *The Nottingham Chronicle*;[66] Peter Gedge of Bury St Edmunds, Suffolk, an agent from 1789,[67] was part owner of *The Bury St. Edmunds and Bury Post*;[68] Clachar, an agent from 1785,[69] was a partner in *The Chelmsford Chronicle*.[70] Other insurance companies followed the pattern established by the Sun; in 1800, James Harrop of Manchester, associated with his father in *Harrop's Manchester Mercury*, and hence with the largest bookselling business in the town, was agent for the British Fire Office.[71]

Medicine selling and insurance agency are conspicuous among the secondary occupations of the provincial booksellers, but there were others. *The Universal British Directory* records, for example, a significant number who were grocers. Some of these may merely have kept a general store in a village, but even here there is a certain logic in the connection. The grocery trade in the eighteenth century was largely concerned with the supply of luxury goods rather than with the basic diet of the urban poor.[72] Despite changing emphasis and the increased sale of proprietary foodstuffs and dry goods, the luxury trade continued to be important.[73] These luxuries included imported products such as tea and sugar. These could be obtained only from central suppliers in London, and again the booksellers were ideally placed to obtain such supplies, and act as provincial outlets for the importers; conversely, grocers were equally well placed to obtain supplies of books.

One other activity deserves special mention, for it was intimately associated with the trade, and many leading booksellers and stationers were involved: the sale of duty stamps. By the end of the eighteenth century, the stamp duties were elaborate and all-embracing; what had begun as a temporary expedient to finance the wars of William III had become one of the bulwarks of the public revenue. There were duties on virtually every kind of documentary transaction from a birth certificate to a death certificate; there were duties on all the means of exchange of money and credit; there were duties on insurance policies, licences, and wills; and there were, of course, duties on newspapers and certain classes of pamphlets.[74] Some attempt was made to rationalise the duties in the last years of George III's reign, but even so Sydney Smith was to complain bitterly of the burden of 'taxes upon every article'.[75]

The stamps were sold by distributors who sent the proceeds to the Commissioners of Stamps, usually quarterly, but often a year or more in arrears, and in the interim the money provided a useful float of liquid capital, a commodity always in short supply in the provinces. They were permitted to charge a fixed percentage for their services, and according to Joseph Hume, radical M.P. for Aberdeen, they made a very good thing of it. Speaking in 1821, he said that the average annual income of a distributor was £1,068, but gave examples of distributors who earned as much as £5,000. At that time there were sixty-eight distributors in England and Wales, but for most of the eighteenth century there were about fifty, a number which had been increased, according to Hume, to give extra government patronage.[76] Certainly the distributorships were sometimes used for political purposes, the most famous example being that of William Wordsworth (an 'indolent poet' according to Hume), but he made only about £200 a year from his office.[77]

In the 1790s, about 40% of all the Stamp Distributors in England and Wales, or about half of those in England, were booksellers. The reasons are not far to seek. By far the greater part of the duties was on documents of various kinds, and these were the very documents which were being sold, either as blank paper or as printed forms, by the booksellers and stationers. When the duties had first been introduced, the London trade had refused to co-operate with the Treasury on the grounds that the profits would be insufficient,[78] but the provincial booksellers of the eighteenth century happily became tax gatherers. Despite the patronage system, a bookseller was in a uniquely strong position to argue his case for a distributorship.[79]

Some of the largest booksellers in the country thought it worth their while to become distributors.[80] Harrop in Manchester was one of them. We can add Swinney, Thomas Pearson, and Thomas Wood in Birmingham, and William Browne in Bristol, all among the larger firms. On the middle level we have Christopher and Jennet in the rapidly growing town of Stockton-on-Tees, where they had the largest bookselling business.[81] William Donaldson, Stamp Distributor in Portsmouth, Hampshire, was the largest bookseller in that town or in nearby Portsea. In Chelmsford, Clachar, inevitably, was the Distributor. In nearby Colchester, however, the situation was slightly different; the Distributor there was Samuel Gibbs, bookseller (and insurance agent), but the largest book-trade business in the town was that of William Keymer, founded in the middle of the century, and remaining in the family until 1821.[82]

The bookshop was a place of great diversity, and the country bookseller could be very different from the ideal described so eloquently by Campbell. There were some well-stocked shops, and some prosperous booksellers, but the majority of those who sold books in the provincial towns needed far more than a good stock of books to make a living. All of them sold stationery, most of them sold patent medicines, a significant number sold insurance, and many leading booksellers and stationers were also Stamp Distributors. In addition, individuals plied many other trades, and sold many other goods. It was a world away from the Temple of the Muses; the bookshop of a small country town was full of paper and bottles and packets of tea, sharing the shelves with Bibles, Prayer Books, chapbooks, school books, and a couple of hundred other volumes, some of them for loan rather than sale. Even many of the larger shops were different from this in degree but not in kind. The chief difference was that a few score of them had one or two wooden presses in a back room or an outhouse on which their owners produced the newspapers which were ultimately responsible for those developments in the trade which brought the printed word and much else to the towns of provincial England.

FINANCE AND PERSONNEL

How did a man become a bookseller? What were the fruits of success and the penalties for failure? What was the social status of these unusual tradesmen?

As in all trades, the easiest means of entry was to succeed to an established family business. George West of Oxford, for example, bequeathed £650 to his three daughters, and the residue of his property, including the bookselling business, to his son in 1704.[83] When the son (also George) made his own will in 1729, the prosperity of the firm had enabled him to purchase an estate at Garsington outside the city.[84]

Marriage was another means of entry and enhancement. The daughter of Henry Hammond, a bookseller in Bath and Devizes from 1695 to 1721, married James Leake, the son of John Leake, a London bookseller whose family business could trace its history back to the reign of Elizabeth I.[85] James was born in 1686, and after three years at Merchant Taylors' was apprenticed in 1702, made free of the Stationers' Company in 1709, and clothed in 1720. His marriage to Hannah Hammond took place in Bath Abbey in the year of her father's death, and Leake immediately inherited the business. It continued to prosper throughout his life, not least through his London connections, which were strengthened when his sister-in-law, Elizabeth, married her father's former apprentice Samuel Richardson in 1733.[86] Leake's will is that of a wealthy man who was able to provide amply for all his family and to leave £10 (more than a year's wages) to one of his employees.[87] The marriage may not have been dynastic, but it certainly did not diminish his fortune.

Marriages between country firms were also common. The daughter of Patrick Sanderson of Durham married Marshall Vesey, a bookseller in Darlington, County Durham, in 1771.[88] This, however, was a bad investment for Vesey; Sanderson went bankrupt in 1778.[89] Another example is provided by the business of the Chases of Norwich. For three generations, from 1715 to 1788, it descended from father to son, with a brief interval from 1744 to 1750 when the widow of the second William was in charge. When the third William had no male heirs, his daughter married Jonathan Matchett, and after his death took William Stevenson as her second husband. Since 1785 Stevenson had been in partnership with another Norwich bookseller, John Crouse. The firm appears in *The Universal British Directory* as Crouse, Stevenson, and Matchett, although the partnership was dissolved, amid some acrimony, in 1796.[90] These family businesses, stable and long-established, were among the most prosperous in the whole trade.

For the aspirant who had no connections through birth or marriage, apprenticeship was the traditional gateway. The apprenticeship system was weakening by the middle of the eighteenth century, and in most cases a man who was practising a trade to which he had not been apprenticed was not in fact prosecuted. There was a marked tendency for boys to remain in their home towns, and, consequently, the proportion gaining freedom by patrimony is high. In Exeter, for example, thirty-five booksellers became Freemen during the century, of whom sixteen reached freedom through patrimony, and a further three by order of the Mayor and Council. Of the sixteen who achieved freedom by apprenticeship, eight did so before 1740, while in the same period only five were freed by patrimony.[91] In York the same picture emerges at an earlier date. Between 1700 and 1740 only six of the twenty-six booksellers who were freed obtained freedom through apprenticeship, while seventeen did so through patrimony. By 1754, only thirteen of the forty-one booksellers freed since the beginning of the century had been apprenticed in their trade.[92]

These are records of freedom, and not all boys proceeded to freedom if they intended to work as journeymen. We can trace some apprenticeships from the registers of stamp duties paid on indentures, a tax which was imposed in 1710.[93] These show that apprenticeship was expensive; the average premium in the trade was just under £20. The master, of course, had more than the money; after a very short time he had, in effect, unpaid labour, which was exactly how White used the young Hansard (p. 27, above). Those who were formally apprenticed were a tiny proportion of all those entering the trade, but they are of some interest. Again the lack of mobility is noticeable; most were apprenticed to a master in their birthplace or the nearest large town. The few who moved further included Clay (Derby to Daventry), John Fancourt of Cornbrooke, Warwickshire (to Cambridge), and William Parkes of Stoke St Milborough, Shropshire (to Worcester). We may suspect business or personal connections as the reasons for these migrations. Sometimes such connections can be documented. Seth Hardy of York was apprenticed to John White in Newcastle-upon-Tyne, but White was the son of a York printer, and still had a branch in the city.[94] Also in York, John Mace was apprenticed to Thomas Ryles of Hull, but he was closely connected with the trade in York as an agent for *The York Courant*.[95]

The record of father's occupation is very sketchy. Of the sixteen (out of 118) for whom it is recorded, one was a gentleman, one an esquire, and three were yeomen. These were the sons of the lesser gentry, although at least one was impoverished as well as gentle; William Cossley's father Richard ('esquire') was able to pay a premium of only £3 to Richard Fawcett of Bristol in 1717. There was one clergyman's son, but all the others were the sons of tradesmen: a baker, a bricklayer, a butcher, a clothmaker, an innholder, a watchmaker, and others. Enough of them, however, came from prosperous backgrounds, if we may judge from the premium, to suggest that the book trade was regarded as a suitable occupation for the son of a family which had successful business experience behind it.

After he had learned his trade a young man could, in theory, choose between working for himself or for someone else, although in practice the choice did not exist for most of them. Setting up in business required a fairly substantial capital, and premises. Shops were often rented, usually it would seem for about £10 per annum for an urban tenement. Henry Clements thought this a fair rent for his shop in Oxford in 1721, and it is typical for most of the century until the great inflation of the 1790s.[96] John Minshull charged ten guineas to a tenant in a similar shop in Chester.[97] In 1762, the small printing office and shop occupied by Samuel Creswell in Nottingham cost him £15.10s.0d. a year.[98]

Stock valuations are more difficult to calculate. We have already used insurance policies for this purpose (p. 73, above), but catalogues can also help. In 1754 Edmund Baker, in the fashionable Kentish spa of Tunbridge Wells, issued a catalogue containing 1,822 items to a total value of £370.15s.0d.[99] It is a typical country catalogue of the period, containing the libraries of two deceased local worthies, and many new books in several fields, most obviously in history, geography, and travels. Comparable catalogues later in the century are those issued by Samuel Tupman in Nottingham in 1790 (1,675 items; £450.17s.9d.), and Ann Ireland in Leicester in 1789 (2,402 items; £274.12s.0d.).[100] In both cases the contents are similar to Baker's catalogue, in Tupman's words 'A Pleasing Variety of Approved Modern Publications, New and Second-Hand'. As much as £5,000 was not too high a capital value for the stock of a large provincial bookseller by the end of the century. In 1789, John Binns of Leeds, in a single catalogue, advertised goods worth over £2,000, of which over £400 was accounted for by pictures, including one each ascribed to Rembrandt and Ruysdael, and nearly £150 by music and instruments, including two harpsichords and two of the recently introduced 'Piano Fortes'.[101] In the middle range, we can select John Burden of Winchester, who insured his books for £1,500 in 1793,[102] or

Joshua Cooke of Oxford, who took out insurance for £800 in the same year.[103]

Stocks of stationery varied even more in size and value. The advertisements, detailed as some of them are, in fact cover wide varieties of sizes and qualities. The stock of William Seale of Oxford, inventoried for probate in 1719, gives a more detailed list of the range of stock held by a stationer.[104] Most of it was writing paper, to a total value of £90.9s.0d. When we consider that his chief occupation was as a bookbinder,[105] we gain some idea of the extent to which a country bookseller could tie up his capital in maintaining the stock of paper which his customers expected to find in his shop. Seale stocked everything listed by Hammond in his advertisement except for wallpaper and mourning paper, and even that may be concealed in the 'old Parcels' and 'loose Paper' at the end of the inventory.

In judging the financial success of eighteenth-century tradesmen, there is probably no better guide than their ownership of property. It conferred social status (p. 30, above), and was one of the few forms of investment readily available. The landowners included Crouse in Norwich,[106] Dagnall of Aylesbury,[107] Easton of Salisbury,[108] Edwards of Halifax,[109] Keymer of Colchester,[110] John Rance of Oxford,[111] West the younger in Oxford,[112] and William Whittingham of King's Lynn, Norfolk.[113] Owners of urban property, in addition to their own houses and shops, included John Blake of Maidstone, Kent,[114] John Blakeney of Windsor,[115] John Brown of Leicester,[116] John Cotton of Shrewsbury,[117] Flackton in Canterbury,[118] Fletcher in Oxford,[119] Benjamin Haydon in Plymouth,[120] Samuel Harward in Cheltenham, Gloucestershire,[121] Thomas Hutton (son of the more famous William) in Birmingham,[122] Merrill in Cambridge,[123] John Padbury in Oxford,[124] Thomas Richard of Plymouth,[125] Thomas Slack of Newcastle-upon-Tyne,[126] James Smith of Newcastle-under-Lyme, Staffordshire,[127] Timothy Stevens of Cirencester, Gloucestershire,[128] and William Turner of Portsmouth.[129] Even comparatively small booksellers made enough money to invest beyond their immediate needs. Other investments were, of course, available to some extent, and a few of the wealthier booksellers took advantage of this (pp. 30–31, above). Such men as these, with funds at their disposal for the purchase of land, houses, and shares, although their wealth was not comparable with that of the great merchants of London and Bristol or that of the new industrial capitalists, were nevertheless men of substance. Cirencester in Gloucestershire, for example, was an ancient town in a rich county, but even in such a place with a tradition of rich merchants a man like Samuel Rudder[130] with £2,000 to invest was to be taken seriously by his fellow citizens. The upward mobility of English society has probably never been more marked than during the years of industrialisation when money could buy both status and power. Tesseyman establishing himself as a country gentleman is unique in the provincial book trade, but the social acceptance of the booksellers in urban communities is everywhere apparent. In Nottingham, for example, two printers were prominent in the city's affairs in the late eighteenth century; Joseph Heath was Chamberlain in 1767, and Sheriff in 1769 and 1789, while George Burbage, the newspaper proprietor, was Chamberlain in 1772, Sheriff in 1773, and a member of the committee which nominated the Mayor in 1793 and 1794.[131]

In many corporate towns there are examples of booksellers following the path from freedom to high office. John Rogers, a bookseller in Shrewsbury from 1707 onwards, was Mayor in 1734;[132] Hammond was Chamberlain of York in 1706;[133] James Simmons of Canterbury held the shrievality of his city in the latter quarter of the century. Simmons, indeed, had a higher political career than any other member of the provincial trade; he became Member of Parliament for Canterbury in 1806.[134] He had already benefited from his political connections; he had used his *Kentish Gazette* in the interest of the Rockingham Whigs, and they made him Distributor of Stamps for Kent during their brief period of office in 1782.[135]

Less orthodox was the political career of Thomas Baker of Southampton. He was one of the leaders of a group which broke the hold of an entrenched oligarchy over the Corporation's affairs between 1791 and 1803. The quarrel concerned the origin and use of the Corporation's revenues, especially those from the Customs. Baker's associates included a banker and other tradesmen to whom the free flow of trade was advantageous.[136] Baker, Simmons, and the others were important men in their communities. A successful bookseller could take his place among the most prominent of his fellow citizens even if he did not aspire to the designation of gentleman.

Status in the community is not to be measured only by civic office. We have already discussed Robert Goadby (pp. 22–23, above), who gave substantial sums to charity. Goadby belonged to the evangelical wing of the Church of England, as did the younger Robert Raikes, owner of *The Gloucester Journal*, who, with Hannah More, was one of the founders of the Sunday School movement. Felix Farley of Bristol bequeathed one guinea to each of the Wesley brothers, whom he described as 'my honoured and much esteemed friends and Pastors'.[137] In Anglican Oxford, it is no surprise that the elder West left 30 shillings to the poor of his parish, St Mary the Virgin, in 1704.[138] William Hutton was a dissenter, well known to be a Unitarian; he suffered for his beliefs when he lost property worth over £8,000 in the notorious Birmingham riots of 1791, in which Joseph Priestley's laboratory was destroyed.[139] Perhaps the most unusual beliefs were those of Samuel Hazard of Bath, who ran a highly successful circulating library and bookshop for over a quarter of a century.[140] Hazard was a member of the Moravians, a sect which had reached England from Germany in the 1730s, and which claimed many followers among the urban middle class. One of the trustees of Hazard's property after his death was Thomas Moore, the 'Bishop' of the Moravians in the west of England.[141] These were men held in high esteem by their co-religionists. It is interesting to note the distinct tendency towards dissent or evangelicalism. This was common among tradesmen, as was its political corollary, Whiggism, conspicuously displayed by Simmons and Baker.

Needless to say, not all booksellers were successful, and towards the end of the century there was a marked increase in the number of bankruptcies (p. 30, above). Even in quite serious cases, however, there was a general desire to avoid the entanglements of the law. On 20 July 1788 Selwin Ramm, an otherwise unrecorded Oxford bookseller, wrote to Thomas Vernor in London to tell him that he was unable to pay for some books which Vernor had supplied. He blamed this on the 'treacherous behaviour of my customers', implying that he had been giving long credit. Vernor's side of the correspondence is lost, but it seems that he was not unsympathetic, for the next letter from Ramm was not written until 28 February 1790. This missive was despatched not from Oxford, whence he had fled to avoid other creditors, but from Woodstock, and in it Ramm coolly informed Vernor that he was able to pay only 1 shilling in the pound. He was in deep trouble, and one can only sympathise with Pierce Walsh who wrote to Vernor in April 1790 that Ramm 'had tried his friends to the last Extremity'. Walsh had taken over Ramm's stock and debts, and was now negotiating with his creditors on his behalf. In June he was able to offer Vernor 5 shillings in the pound, and to hold out the hope of another 5 shillings, although this, he admitted, was 'uncertain'.[142] The significance of this little story is that despite the extent of Ramm's indebtedness, his prevarications, his apparent inability to pay, and his unwillingness to make realistic offers of settlement, there seems to have been no suggestion of recourse to the Court of Chancery with its interminable delays and unpredictable costs.

It is clear from other cases that formal bankruptcy proceedings were started only when very substantial sums were involved. When Robert Christopher of Stockton-on-Tees, County Durham, found himself in difficulties in 1797, he avoided proceedings by mortgaging his property to Thomas Jennet, his former apprentice, who now became his partner.[143]

Thomas Warren of Birmingham was perhaps the the most spectacular failure of the first half of the century. He was in Birmingham in 1727, and two years later was undertaking book printing.[144] He started the town's first newspaper, *The Birmingham Journal*, probably in November 1732.[145] Samuel Johnson lodged with Warren, and wrote some pieces, which have not survived, for his newspaper; it was also at Warren's suggestion that Johnson undertook his first major work, the translation of Lobo's *Voyage to Abyssinia*, published in 1735.[146] When Warren was in financial difficulties in the 1740s Johnson tried to help him, and acted as intermediary between him and some of his creditors.[147]

Warren's difficulties did not arise from his activities in the book trade; indeed, as a newspaper owner in a growing town he was ideally placed for a successful career. The problems arose from Warren's dealings with Lewis Paul, the inventor of a spinning machine which he patented in 1738. To support his work, which included the building of the first spinning mill, Paul borrowed heavily, and in 1740 he owed Warren £1,000. Warren no doubt saw this as an investment, but Paul could not repay the money; instead he offered to give Warren the right to sell fifty of the spindles which were the crucial part of the invention. By now, however, Warren himself was seriously short of money. By March 1741, he had lost his credit with the London booksellers. Warren wrote desperately to Paul: 'if I can't . . . make a Cred[t] for Ten or Twenty Pounds, I must at all events shut up my Shop'.[148] To make matters worse, Paul had used the good offices of Warren and Johnson to obtain money from others, including Edward Cave of *The Gentleman's Magazine*[149] and Dr James, inventor of the Fever Powder. When Paul was made bankrupt in 1742, Warren was brought down with him.[150] Warren's bankruptcy was formalised on

3 January 1743,[151] and his assignees auctioned his share in the spindles.[152] The proceeds of this sale enabled Warren to re-establish his business, which then prospered until his death in 1767 and continued into the nineteenth century.[153]

Warren's bankruptcy arose from a foolish investment outside the book trade. It is noteworthy that his activities in the trade had produced enough money within a dozen years for him to be able to invest £1,000. The impression is that Warren was an ambitious man with an expanding business.

Caesar Ward of York, another bankrupt in the first half of the century, was also the victim of bad judgement. From about 1734 he was in partnership with Richard Chandler, who had moved from York to London in 1732. During the 1730s they were partners in *The York Courant*, although Chandler dropped out in about 1740. By that time he was in serious debt, and 'rather than become a despicable object to the world, or bear the miseries of a prison, he put a period to his life, by discharging a pistol into his head'. Chandler's suicide was in 1744; within eighteen months Ward was bankrupt. The cause of both the suicide and the bankruptcy was Chandler's ambitious undertaking to publish a twelve-volume *History and proceedings of the House of Commons from the Restoration* (London, 1741–43); as Gent put it, Chandler's 'thoughts soared too high, and sunk his fortunes so low, by the debts he had contracted'. Like Warren, Ward was a prosperous bookseller brought to bankruptcy by imprudence and the misjudgement of a partner; like Warren, he recovered, and his firm survived until the nineteenth century.[154]

Warren and Ward are typical of the bankruptcies in the provincial book trade. Where we can add some details to the mere fact of bankruptcy, there is a common theme of over-ambition and unsuccessful competition with an established rival. Christopher Etherington had been in the trade in York for fourteen years when, in 1772, he bought some presses and started *The York Chronicle*. Even a city of the importance of York could not support two newspapers, and Etherington was unable to compete with the long-established *York Courant*. He went bankrupt in January 1777, and vanished from the trade. The title of his newspaper, ironically, was later revived, this time successfully.[155] In Sherborne, Dorset, William Cruttwell tried to compete with Goadby's *Western Flying Post*. From 1765 he published *Cruttwell's Sherborne Journal* as a Tory competitor to Goadby's Whig paper. The market could not sustain him, however, and in October

1778 he went bankrupt. Like so many others, he recovered from his misfortune; the business survived in the family until 1824,[156] and Cruttwell himself left a substantial fortune which included a farm in Somerset.[157]

Not all bankrupts returned to the book trade. James Linden of Southampton, whose bankruptcy was gazetted in February 1778, was one of two booksellers in the town, competing against Baker, the scourge of the Corporation (p. 92, above). They competed strongly for the circulating-library business in an increasingly popular seaside resort, and it was Linden who succumbed. After his bankruptcy Linden abandoned the book trade, and concentrated on his other enterprises including an Academy for Young Gentlemen which he had helped to start in 1773.[158]

All of these went bankrupt through their own errors. That was not the case of the unfortunate William Charnley of Newcastle-upon-Tyne. Charnley had been trained by, and was subsequently in partnership with, Martin Bryson, who had been in business in the town since 1726. When Bryson retired in 1755, Charnley took over a flourishing bookshop, which he expanded by starting a circulating library in 1757. His shop was on the ancient bridge over the Tyne and was destroyed, along with his entire stock, when the bridge was swept away in a great flood in 1771. He tried to recover his fortunes; what was left of the circulating library was sold to Richard Fisher,[159] but even so he went bankrupt in February 1773.[160] Ironically, his trade was already reviving, and having paid his debts he went back into business. His widow, son, and grandson followed him as booksellers, and the firm outlived the disaster by 110 years, ceasing to trade in 1881.[161]

These failures would be the wrong note on which to end this chapter, although no account of provincial bookselling would be complete without them. The overwhelming evidence is that most booksellers were modestly successful, and a few outstandingly so. They sold a great variety of goods, many of which, like books, were among the small number dependent upon centralised distribution from London. In 1700, such goods were very unusual; by 1800 they were less so, although the changing structure of the country's economic geography meant that goods were as likely to come from Lancashire or the Potteries as they were from the capital. In essence, however, the book distribution system, and the associated patterns of advertising and sale of other goods, survived into the early nineteenth century and was not seriously disrupted until the building of the railways revolutionised the distributive trades in the 1840s. The bookselling business was diverse and complex; in the right hands it could also be a source of both status and profit.

CHAPTER 6

The Printing Office

In 1733 Thomas Gent was generous to his nephew, Arthur Clarke. He set him up in business in the popular resort of Scarborough on the Yorkshire coast, where he was the first printer. Clarke's shop became something of a tourist attraction: 'The gentry from the Spa used to visit us, to have their names, and see the playhouse bills and other work printed.'[1] Clarke's printing house was not alone in receiving such attention. While presses were still unusual in the provinces they were often visited by the curious. Nicholas Blundell of Little Crosby, Lancashire, recorded in his diary for 5 July 1712 that he had visited Samuel Terry's printing house when he was in nearby Liverpool.[2] Terry was the first Liverpool printer, and had been in business for only a few weeks; the first issue of his *Leverpoole Courant* had probably appeared on 12 May.[3] Later in the century, the printing trade was sufficiently widespread to be less interesting, and as we have seen by about 1770 there were few towns of any size without at least one printer. The activities of these printers were very varied: some produced newspapers, some produced books, all did jobbing work, and most of them were also booksellers and stationers. The key role of the newspaper printers in the trade has already been discussed at some length, but in this chapter we shall open the door to the printing office itself. What equipment and materials were to be found there? How many men were at work? What were the costs, charges, and profits of the provincial printer? What did he print, and how did he sell it?

EQUIPMENT, MATERIALS, AND WORKERS

The basic equipment of the printer was the press itself, and the type, together with the various essential accessories such as chases, furniture, and inking apparatus. Surprisingly little is known about the manufacture of the wooden press which was universal throughout the eighteenth century. Pendred gives the names of three printers' joiners and two printers' brokers in London.[4] Two of the joiners are otherwise unknown, but we have a little information about James Arding of

Shoe Lane. Pendred's *Vade Mecum* is the first record of him, but his firm survived for eighty years after 1785.[5] Thomas Cheney, son of John, knew of him in 1805, and names him with two other printers' joiners and pressmakers in a list of London suppliers which he compiled when he took over the family business in that year.[6] A fourth pressmaker was John Collins of Winchester Yard, Borough, in south London; he was in business at least from 1780 to 1795.[7]

Pressmaking was a specialised activity, and Cheney's interest shows that the provincial printers were aware of the services offered by the London manufacturers. It seems possible that some provincial printers dealt through the brokers, who acted as middlemen. No provincial example can be quoted, but the activities of Harrild and Sons as printers' brokers is well known from the part they played in the history of the press alleged to have been used by Benjamin Franklin.[8] Cheney noted the names of two London brokers in his list of suppliers; they were James Fricker, of Leadenhall Street,[9] and 'W. Kemmis', probably William Kemmish of Southwark.[10]

In the first half of the century, however, we know little of individual pressmakers or brokers, although we do know that there were specialised joiners in London. Moxon implies this when he says of 'the Old-fashion'd *Presses*' that 'the demensions of every particular Member I shall omit, referring those that think it worth their while, to the *Joyners* and *Smiths* that work to *Printers*'.[11] In 1713, James Watson wrote that until recently presses came from Holland, but that 'of late Years' they had been made in London, although he implied that the English presses were inferior to the Dutch, and not of the latest design.[12] Moxon gave full details of the 'New-fashion'd *Press*', from which it would have been possible to build one.[13] Apart from the rather complicated screw of the Blaeu hose, there is nothing in a wooden press which could not have been made by any competent carpenter, and some presses may have been built in the provinces in this way. At least one provincial printing firm took an interest in pressmaking. Isaac Moore and William Pine of Bristol developed a new lever mechanism, which they patented in 1771, and a number of small presses were built to their design.[14]

A printer could function with a single press, and some provincial printers may have done so. For newspaper work, however, more were sometimes used. As early as the 1720s, John White, printer of *The York Courant*, had three presses.[15] In 1799, Myles Swinney, printer of *Swinney's Birmingham Chronicle*, had four presses; T. A. Pearson,

Swinney's rival, and printer of *Aris's Birmingham Gazette*, had five. No other Birmingham printer had more than two presses, and none elsewhere in Warwickshire more than one.[16] Other scraps of evidence confirm that the newspaper printers normally had more than two presses. William Pine, the Bristol printer and owner of *The Bristol Gazette*, referred in his will to his 'machines', although this probably included some of the presses which he and Moore had built.[17] A few of the larger printers who had no newspaper also had more than one press; in an inventory probably compiled in 1788, John Cheney listed two presses.[18]

The cost of a press increased slowly through the century, but second-hand presses, which were much cheaper, seem to have been readily available. In 1702, the Curators of Cambridge University Press paid £11.11s.0d. for a second-hand press.[19] John White's presses were valued for probate at only £5.0s.0d. each; Cheney valued his at £12.10s.0d. New presses were more expensive. Oxford University Press paid £17.3s.9d. for a press from Yalloly, a London pressmaker, in 1767.[20] In the 1780s, the proprietors of *The Gazetteer* paid £20.0s.0d. each for two presses.[21] In the 1790s, the Frenchman Silvestre Bouchard costed a new press at the equivalent of £19.1s.0d.[22] In 1808, Caleb Stower gave the cost of a 'Common' printing press (that is, a wooden press) as £31.10s.0d.[23]

Although the presses were the largest pieces of equipment in the printing office, far more money was invested in type. Cheney had nearly 2,500 lb, in eighty-four cases; White seems to have had twenty-one cases of type. Cheney's largest quantities were of Pica, of which he had altogether some 1,200 lb. Moxon had recommended that a small printer needed 800 to 1,000 lb of Pica, 500 lb of Long Primer (Cheney had 231 lb), 800 to 1,000 lb of English (489½ lb), 100 lb of Great Cannon (116 lb), and 300 to 400 lb of other types and symbols, flowers and rules.[24] This would have cost about £300 at the end of the seventeenth century,[25] and approximately twice that by 1800.[26] The significant fact is that Cheney valued one press at about 9% of the total value of his type. One of White's presses was valued at rather less than 5% of his type (£5.0s.0d. as against £105.0s.0d.). This is a measure of the heavy investment which a printer made in buying his types.

Only one provincial printer's type specimen is extant from the eighteenth century, from outside the University presses. It was issued by W. H. Parker of Hereford; it is probably to be dated about 1800, although Parker had been printing in the city since 1784.[27] The *Specimen*, which may be fragmentary, shows a similar range of type to that owned by Cheney. There are two designs of English, and one each of Pica, Long Primer, Double Pica, Great Primer, Two-line Double Pica, and Two-line English. Italic is shown only for Pica, Long Primer, and Double Pica. In addition, there are flowers in all these sizes except Double Pica and the two-line English, and a number of ornaments including two Royal Arms. We do not, of course, know how much type Parker actually had, but the *Specimen* can be taken as typical of the variety of type available in a provincial printing office at the end of the century.

Typefounding, like pressmaking, was largely but not entirely confined to London. Pendred lists six London typefounders[28] but none in the provinces, and none is listed in *The Universal British Directory*. Types were, however, made at both Oxford and Cambridge, and Baskerville's first types were cut and, apparently, made in Birmingham.[29] It seems that Birmingham, with its multiplicity of small craft industries, was something of a centre of typefounding. George Anderton was making types there in 1753,[30] and later printers in the city, Robert Martin (c.1780),[31] and Myles Swinney (c.1790 to at least 1801),[32] were also typefounders. Isaac Moore of Bristol, the printer and pressmaker, was a typefounder there in 1766, but he subsequently moved to London.[33] Thomas Cheney's list of suppliers, however, gives the names only of five London foundries.[34] Had Cheney been further north the situation might have been different. Many books printed in Newcastle-upon-Tyne, especially the great output of chapbooks, are in types which appear to be of Scottish origin. This would certainly be consistent with what were obviously very close links between the trades in Scotland and on Tyneside.

The men who used the type and presses included the proprietors themselves in most printing houses, but all except the very smallest firms had employees, while the newspaper printers had substantial staffs. No provincial printer ever employed the great numbers of workmen to be found in the major London printing houses, but two or three men were quite usual. Stephen White of Norwich had one full-time and one part-time journeyman in the late 1760s, as well as his apprentice Luke Hansard,[35] but some establishments were larger. In 1778, Goadby had three journeymen and an apprentice,[36] and we may take this as typical of the newspaper office.

Unlike the booksellers, the printers needed specific expertise, although in the small office the journeyman was expected to be a jack of all work like Hansard. In 1780, Ann Cox of Grantham, Lincolnshire, advertised for 'A Journeyman, that can print, and bind'.[37] In larger offices, however, there were specialists. In 1781, Daniel Prince of Oxford recommended Joseph Pardon to John Nichols; Pardon, he wrote, was 'a good Hand at the Case, & can also be useful at the Press'. He 'would be glad of Business in London', having been 'bred up' there.[38] A good compositor was always in demand, and the tramping system, which was to be so familiar in the nineteenth century,[39] was already feasible by the 1760s or 1770s. At about that time Charles Rathband spent some years on the tramp. He worked on newspapers in Canterbury, Chester, and Hereford, and was unusual only in contributing to *The Gentleman's Magazine*, and in ending his career as editor of *The General Evening Post*.[40]

The provincial printing office was small, but adequate for its owner's purposes. Goadby, for example, certainly had enough men to keep two presses in continuous use, and to have had plenty of capacity to produce books and jobbing work as well as his newspaper. Like other proprietors, he spread the load of the newspaper printing through the week.[41] In six ten-hour days, a printer with two presses had a very large potential output. Despite the small size of the firms, the provincial printers were well able to produce not only their newspaper, but also the handbills, posters, ballad sheets, and chapbooks which were the mainstay of their trade.

COSTS AND PROFITS

The printer's costs, apart from initial expenditure on equipment and premises, were made up of materials and wages. Paper was bought from the mills, although stamped paper for newspapers had to come from London, which occasionally caused delays.[42] Indeed, the cost of stamped paper was a major item in the newspaper printer's expenditure.

Our knowledge of wages is fragmentary until the end of the century. By 1800, a London compositor earned 5d. an hour (£1.16s.0d. a week) according to Francis Place,[43] but the rates varied according to the work in hand. The London Scale of Prices, first drawn up in 1785, regulated the wages of both compositors and pressmen, the former in terms of type size and ems set, with rather higher rates for newspaper work.[44] It has been suggested that the provincial journeymen reached parity with their London brethren towards the end of the century,[45] a suggestion which is confirmed by Thomas Cheney's interest in the London Scale. He wrote a copy of the 1805 Scale in his memorandum book.[46] Earlier in the century, wages were lower. Goadby seems to have paid his journeymen about 4s.0d. a week, for he bequeathed £10.0s.0d. to each of them as the equivalent of a year's wages.[47] James Leake of Bath was paying £20.0s.0d. a year to his foreman, William Taylor, in 1760.[48] If the men were paid according to the London Scale by 1800 this represented a significant improvement.

The charges made to customers are equally difficult to calculate, although again there are scraps of evidence. In his first account book, Cheney noted the quantities he printed; unfortunately, his later ledgers are simply records of customers' accounts. A few examples from 1769 and 1770 are, however, useful as a guide to his charges for jobbing work. They were not entirely uniform, and probably varied according to difficulty. For example, in June 1770 he charged Richard Wagstaffe of Chipping Norton 6s.6d. for one handbill in 400 copies, but only 5s.6d. for the same quantity of three others. Another customer was charged 3s.6d. for 300 handbills for an auction sale, but Robert Osborne, an ironmonger in Banbury, was charged only 3s.7d. for 540 handbills, presumably on half- or quarter-sheets.[49] Prices, however, were subject to great variation. In 1742, William Ayres of Winchester charged the City Council no less than £1.1s.0d. for only forty-one copies of the single sheet of Orders and Rules to be obeyed by the city's officers.[50]

Book printing is an even more contentious area. Blackstone maintained that the country printers tried to woo customers away from the London trade by charging lower prices.[51] Given the structure of the trade, this is inherently improbable, but Blackstone's statement, for which he gave no evidence, is in any case quite impossible to assess, since we know so little about London prices before the end of the century. An elaborate attempt to calculate William Strahan's 'standard charges'[52] has been seriously challenged,[53] and we can really do little more than select specific examples of provincial practices. Charges were by the sheet and the number of copies printed, but again type size and the difficulty of setting were large factors in establishing the price. In 1752, the Welsh poet Goronwy Owen wrote that the standard price in Shrewsbury was 'two guineas a sheet for 1,000 copies', but as this was for Welsh printing there may have been additional charges for difficulty. In 1771, Benjamin Collins of

Salisbury charged £1.6s.od. a sheet for 1,500 copies of *Humphry Clinker*,[54] a rare example of a provincial printer undertaking what would normally have been London work. Collins also printed the first edition of *The Vicar of Wakefield*,[55] but he was uniquely well connected to the London trade (p. 4, above) and is atypical. His charge for Smollett's book could be compared with Strahan's £1.2s.od. a sheet for 1,000 copies of Ossian's *Works* in 1774,[56] but such comparisons are not very helpful in the light of our ignorance of 'standard charges' and the distinct possibility that they did not exist. By the end of the century, however, the acceptance of the London Scale as a guide enforced a degree of standardisation.[57]

Profits can be measured only by the wealth of the printers, and their own estimates of the value of their businesses. Nothing resembling a profit-and-loss account can be compiled from any surviving documents. Successful newspapers were, of course, the most profitable part of the printing trade. When Robert Raikes the younger sold *The Gloucester Journal* to Walker of Hereford in 1802, part of the agreement between them was that Raikes should have an annuity of £300 a year from the profits of the paper.[58] Richard Cruttwell wrote in 1797 that 'The property of the Bath Chronicle I estimate at £4000', and he envisaged that his estate would pay one annuity of £200 and four of £250 from the profits.[59] Goadby was so convinced of the value of *The Western Flying Post* that he forbade his heirs to sell it, so that they could pay his bequests out of the income.[60] A more modest business like Cheney's produced more modest profits, but even they were a sufficient basis for long-term survival and success.

JOBBING WORK

The common denominator of all provincial printers was that they relied heavily on jobbing work. In the years immediately after 1695 there is ample evidence that jobbing was already widely practised by the pioneer printers. The Common Council of Bristol clearly envisaged that Bonny would undertake such work (p. 2, above), and we know that Darker was printing blank forms for apprenticeship indentures in Exeter before the end of the seventeenth century.[61] In 1721, Bagnall in Ipswich was advertising that he did jobbing work,[62] and in 1728 John Collyer of Nottingham printed tickets and programmes for the Corporation.[63] All of these men were newspaper proprietors, but by the middle of the century a printer without a newspaper could make a good income from jobbing work (pp. 26–27, above). In the last quarter of the century, jobbing work in the industrial areas became very important. *The Universal British Directory* records, for example, that John Varden of Bilston in the west midlands was a specialist box printer.

Cheney's ledger from the 1790s[64] gives a vivid picture of the work of the jobbing printer and the extent to which printing had become an integral part of the social and economic life of the provinces. Cheney's work was conditioned by the economic life of Banbury and the surrounding villages, which was primarily agricultural. As a consequence, a high proportion of the printing was of auctioneers' bills and catalogues, for sales of land, farms, stock, crops, and timber. The largest single customer was the auctioneer Joseph Hawtyn, who spent £110.9s.3d. between 22 February 1794 and 9 December 1800, all of it for auction catalogues and posters. Hawtyn had a large business of which auctioneering was only a part; he was also a wholesale brazier, an occupation which required substantial capital.[65] Cheney's second largest customer was Thomas Young of Banbury, whom Cheney described as a 'papermaker'. He spent £102.11s.6d. between 21 March 1794 and 8 February 1800, over half of it (£62.9s.4d.) on 'Copper Plate Work'; the commissions were chiefly for ream and bale labels. It is not clear who Young was; if he was a Banbury man, as Cheney's accounts state, he must have been at North Newington which, some three miles away, was the only mill near the town, the next nearest being at Deddington, six miles to the south on the Oxford road. John Jones was at North Newington from 1756 to 1778; after 1792, the mill was in the hands of three partners, Thomas Cobb, John Pain, and William Judd, all Banbury men and all customers of Cheney, but its occupancy from 1778 to 1792 is unknown.[66] Possibly Young was the partners' manager, or the master papermaker at the mill. Cheney's third largest customer was Richard Bignall. He was a lawyer, and later a banker,[67] but he also seems to have been an auctioneer, for his orders included posters and bills of sale, as well as legal documents such as subpoenas and warrants, and other blank forms. Probably he arranged for the sale of his clients' goods and property. Bignall was a leading man in local affairs; it was he, for example, who chose the architect for the new parish church in the late 1780s, and it was he also who drafted the private Bill which sought permission to demolish the existing building.[68]

These three provided over half of Cheney's printing orders in the last seven years of the eighteenth century, and his other customers were all on a much smaller scale. Auctioneers and lawyers are notable among them. The former included Thacker and Carter of Banbury, Harris of Bicester, possibly DeChare of Horley, William Holtham of Chipping Norton, and possibly others. Of the lawyers we can certainly identify William Walford and Oliver Aplin, both of Banbury, and a Mr Thomas of Brackley.

Other occupations, however, also provided work for Cheney. The Oxford Canal was opened throughout from Coventry to Oxford via Banbury in 1790,[69] and several of Cheney's customers were involved with it. Simcock and Sebridge of Heyford and Aynho had four guineas' worth of tickets printed for them between 1795 and 1802; both villages are on the Canal, and it seems certain that Simcock and Sebridge were carriers. The same was true of Hunt of Aynho Wharf, who paid £13.12s.6d. for tickets between 1795 and 1799, and of James Golby of Castle Wharf, Banbury, who had tickets printed at a cost of £2.14s.0d. in 1796 and 1797. James Wood of Lower Heyford may have been a carrier on the roads, and William Judd of Banbury certainly was.[70] Judd had a large business, including regular waggon services to London and Birmingham. Cheney also produced stationery for Richard Wagstaffe, the Phoenix Fire Office agent at Chipping Norton; tickets for the Banbury Bridge toll for Mr Thomas of Brackley, who was the lessee; medicine labels for Marriott, a Banbury druggist; miscellaneous stationery for Cobb and Cobb of Banbury Old Bank; playbills for an actor called Watson, who brought his company from Cheltenham for a visit to Banbury in 1798; and notices for the Banbury Prosecuting Society which tried to defend the town against criminals, and the Banbury Armed Association which proposed to defend it against Napoleon.[71] By the end of the century, Cheney's printing office was an essential part of the fabric of Banbury's commercial life, and of that of an area extending for about fifteen miles around the town. Similar printers were scattered throughout the country, producing work of the same kind.

BALLAD SHEETS, CHAPBOOKS, AND ALMANACS

Newspapers, ballad sheets, and chapbooks constituted the second largest part of the output of the provincial printing trade after jobbing work. As Cranfield and Wiles have both dealt at length with the printing of newspapers[72] there is little point in discussing it here. Its importance is obvious from previous chapters; but it ought to be remembered that its importance was out of all proportion to the actual number of newspaper printers. Even at the end of the century there were fewer than a hundred newspapers in the provinces, and many of them were of very recent origin.

By contrast, the history of provincial ballad and chapbook printing has been sadly neglected. This is hardly surprising, for there are few ballads and chapbooks extant, and many of those which are have undated imprints. The greatest centre of chapbook printing outside London was Newcastle-upon-Tyne, where the tradition was started by John White in about 1712. White's partner and successor, Thomas Saint, carried on this aspect of the business, and from the mid 1770s a second firm, that of Thomas Angus, who was succeeded by his widow and his son, also entered the market. Angus surpassed even White in the quantity of chapbooks which he produced.[73] It is significant that many of the Newcastle chapbooks and ballads have a distinctly Scottish flavour, for a large number of them made their way northwards, although there was also a huge potential market to the south among the industrial towns of County Durham. John Catnach, who, at Berwick in 1790 and afterwards at Alnwick, was a large-scale printer of chapbooks, especially for children, was himself a Scot, and like the Newcastle printers he had close contacts with the Scottish book trade.[74] It seems certain that the Scottish market was an important element in the economy of the book trade in Northumberland; the close links are confirmed by the dealing between Charnley in Newcastle and Kincaid and Bell in Edinburgh.[75]

Another major centre of chapbook production was Northampton, where William Dicey, co-founder of *The Northampton Mercury*, began printing them in the early 1720s.[76] It seems possible that Dicey had been involved in the chapbook trade in London before moving into the country with Robert Raikes, and that he was in fact printing texts which were protected until 1731–32 when the pre-1710 copyrights expired. Certainly his son, Cluer, moved back to London in the mid 1730s, and it has been suggested[77] that this was because the Diceys could now print legally the books which they had formerly pirated. The Diceys' business in Aldermary Churchyard, London, flourished for many years, but William, the father, continued to print chapbooks at Northampton until his death in 1756. Dicey may not have been the only pirate. J. Bence of Wootton-under-Edge, Gloucestershire, printed *Robinson Crusoe* and other texts, perhaps as early as

1725. Unless the imprint was false, which is improbable, there seems little reason for a printer to be in so obscure a place unless to evade the law.[78]

Associated with chapbook printing was the printing of ballad sheets, which was common throughout the provincial trade. There were some specialists, like Cheney,[79] but most printers produced some. White of Norwich was one of them;[80] another was William Eyres of Warrington, Cheshire, better known as a printer of works of learning in elegant quarto volumes.[81] Clay bought both ballads and chapbooks from several printers, including Thomas Luckman and J. W. Piercy, rival newspaper printers in Coventry, and the more obscure Francis Makepeace of Southam, Warwickshire.[82] In Salisbury, from about 1770 to the end of the century, E. Fowler printed hundreds of ballads similar in style and subject-matter to the thousands printed throughout the country.[83]

Fowler's ballads include many on local themes such as the rebuilding of Salisbury Council House in 1785;[84] in this he was typical. The ballads and chapbooks were designed primarily for a local market, and hence distribution was comparatively simple. The newsagents and newsmen were, as ever, prominent in this trade, as can be seen from this imprint of a Dicey ballad:[85]

Northampton: Printed by Wm. Dicey, and sold at Mr. Burnham's Snuff-shop, and by Mathias Dagnall Bookseller in Aylesbury; Paul Stevens in Bicester; Wm. Ratten Bookseller in Coventry; Caleb Ratten Bookseller in Harborough; Tho. Williams Bookseller in Tring; Anthony Thorpe in St. Albans; Wm. Peachey near St. Bennet's Church in Cambridge; Mary Timbs in Newport-pagnell; John Timbs in Stony-Stratford; Jer. Rose in Derby; John Hirst Printer in Leeds; and by Churrode Brady in St. Ives. All at which Places Chapmen and Travellers may be furnish'd with the best sort of Old and new Ballads Broadsheets, &c.

Some of the booksellers were agents for *The Northampton Mercury*, including Dagnall, Stevens, and the Rattens. Others were useful regional contacts; John Hirst, for example, was the owner of *The Leeds Mercury*.[86] The booksellers, however, were not merely selling the ballads and chapbooks at their shops or through newsmen. They were also acting as local wholesalers, supplying the 'Chapmen and Travellers'. These men, the last of the itinerant booksellers, were crucial to the ballad and chapbook trade everywhere throughout the century, and it was they who ensured that the thousands of songs and penny histories found their way into every village in England.

Only one other category of book achieved the popularity of the ballad sheets and chapbooks: the almanacs. The huge circulation of the almanacs made them an obvious area of interest for the provincial printers, but there was a major complication. Since 1603, the right to print almanacs had been vested in the Stationers' Company. During the seventeenth century the almanac monopoly had become a vital part of the English Stock from which the Company derived much of its income.[87] After 1695, however, control of the almanac monopoly became increasingly difficult, and there was a good deal of provincial piracy, especially after about 1740. The formal attack on the monopoly was led by Thomas Carnan, son of the Reading printer William Carnan, who owned *The Reading Mercury*.[88] His stepfather was John Newbery, who had also started his career in Reading, and who, as we have seen (p. 84, above), had wide provincial contacts through both his book and his medicine trades. Carnan challenged the Company in the courts, and the House of Lords, influenced by their own decision in *Miller* v. *Donaldson*, ruled the monopoly illegal in 1775.

Carnan's provincial links are significant. Having been brought up in the provincial trade, he knew that such books could be printed and sold in the provinces as the chapbooks were, and that they were potentially very profitable. In fact, the famous London almanacs, such as Old Moore, survived the destruction of the monopoly, but many provincial printers did produce local almanacs in the last twenty years of the century. Like the chapbooks, they were sold by pedlars as well as booksellers.

Almanacs, ballads, and chapbooks were a very important part of the provincial printer's work, and were by far the largest category of provincially printed 'books'. The market was so large that a printer's local distribution network could give him enough sales to make the enterprise worthwhile. With other books, however, he had the problem of seeking a national market from a local base, and it is to that problem, and its partial solution, that we shall now direct our attention.

BOOK PRINTING AND PUBLISHING

Parson Adams was not, so far as his creator reveals, intimately acquainted with the structure and organisation of the book trade; but he knew enough to take his sermons to London so that they would be properly published and have a wide circulation.[89] The attitude was a common one. Laurence Sterne tried desperately to persuade Dodsley to publish *Tristram Shandy*, and only when he refused was the book printed in York. The shame of its provincial origin was concealed in an imprint which reads '1760'.[90] The other great literary work of the century published – as opposed to being merely printed – in the provinces was a commercial catastrophe. *Lyrical Ballads*, printed and published by Joseph Cottle in Bristol, was instrumental in the failure of its publisher, and the whole edition was sold to John and Arthur Arch in London within five days of publication.[91] The distribution system, revolving around the contacts between the London trade and the regional distributors, especially the newspaper owners, militated strongly against provincial publishing on an economic scale.

Authors whose books were printed locally were generally those whose appeal was only to a local market. There was a good deal of vanity publishing, much of it by clergymen in search of preferment. An early example is the anonymous *Paraphrase on the XXVIII Chapter of Deuteronomy*:

Chester: Printed by W.ᵐ Cooke; for the Author. MDCCXXIII.

Some years later, John Sedgfield's *Jeohovah Tsidkenu; or, a discourse on that glorious title of Jesus Christ* had this imprint:

Kendal, Printed by Tho. Ashburner, 1736.

In 1789, John Baillie's *Vindication of the divinity of Jesus Christ* was 'Published by Desire':

Newcastle: Printed by Hall and Elliot, 1789.

Conventional theology was not the only class of literature published in this way. Coleridge's *Moral and political lecture* (1795) was another example:

Bristol: Printed by George Routh, in Corn-street.

A schoolmaster, Benjamin Rhodes, failed to achieve the desired immortality with his *Concise English grammar*:

Birmingham: Printed by J. Belcher, 1795.

Such imprints say nothing of arrangements for distribution; there were none. The book was sold by the printer and the author, often having been printed at the author's expense. These simple imprints indicate that a book could never have had more than a very restricted local circulation. Some books were indeed designed for that purpose, most obviously the guide books. *A description of Brighthelmstone*, for example (p. 70, above), had this imprint:

Brighthelmstone: Printed for A. Crawford.

An interesting but not unique variant is Henry Coward's *New description of the pictures, statues, bustos, basso relievos, and other curiosities, in the earl of Pembroke's house, at Wilton*:

Salisbury: Printed by E. Easton, for Henry Coward, at Wilton-House. M. DCC. LXXXIX.

Coward was employed at Wilton as a guide for the many visitors who came to see the famous Pembroke collections. He took his job seriously; his book, for which he charged 2s.6d., was merely an introduction to a tour which at least one distinguished visitor found as exhausting as it was exhaustive.[92]

Just as London books with a specific regional interest had named regional distributors (pp. 64–67, above), so a provincial printer who sought a national market reversed the process by finding a London distributor, or, in contemporary trade parlance, a 'publisher'. In 1783, B. C. Collins of Salisbury discussed the problem in a letter to Nichols:[93]

A Publisher is quite requisite. I know of none more eligible than Mr Baldwin Booksr in the Row – a happy Collation of Industry, Integrity, and Method. For these weighty Reasons I have given him the preferance and as your Letter will amply explain the Business have taken the Liberty to inclose it to him –.

The implication is that Nichols and Collins, who were publishing the book jointly, were conferring a privilege on Baldwin by allowing him to distribute it. William Johnstone told the Commons in 1775 that 'wholesale booksellers in London, solicit the country booksellers to supply them with books', but this has to be seen in the context of the debate on the booksellers' Copyright Bill, where it was to their advantage to show that the London trade was dependent upon the country trade.[94] Indeed it was, but not in the way Johnstone implied, for the dependence was on the country booksellers as distributors, not as suppliers.

Collins knew the London trade well; indeed, few country booksellers were as deeply involved in it as he. He was well able, perhaps uniquely well able, to select a wholesaler for his publications, for he had the right contacts, and the London booksellers knew that he was sound. A less well-connected, and less prosperous, country bookseller was faced with a greater problem. William Harrod was always in financial difficulties. He was a printer and bookseller in various parts of the east midlands, starting in Stamford in the 1780s, moving to Mansfield by 1801, and returning to Market Harborough, his birthplace, where his father had also been a printer and bookseller, in 1805. He died, in poverty, in Birmingham in 1819.[95] He printed four of his own antiquarian works: *The history and antiquities of Stamford and St Martins* in 1785; two parts only of *Wright's Antiquities of Rutland, with additions . . . by W. Harrod* in 1788; *The history of Mansfield and its environs* in 1801; and *The history of Market-Harborough* in 1808.

On 3 June 1801, when *The history of Mansfield* was almost ready for publication, he wrote to John Nichols:[96]

The work is entirely printed, excepting the Title page, not having determined upon a Books[r] in London. I wish you would mention one who is willing to do the business.

On 12 August, he wrote again:[97]

I shall finish printing this next week . . . please to say if I may add your name, as Vender in London or not? If not, I shall be glad if you will send me the name of any eminent Books[r] who is agreeable to sell it.

In the end, Nichols agreed to distribute the book, and duly appears in the imprint:

Mansfield: Printed and sold by its author. Sold also in London by Mr. Nichols, Red Lion Passage, Fleet Street, and Messrs. F. and C. Rivington. 1801.

Harrod had his London contacts, but even so he seems to have had some difficulty in persuading Nichols to be his distributor.

The London bookseller was also expected to advise on, and to arrange for, the advertisements in the London newspapers which were so necessary for a book's success. Harrod's letters to Nichols are instructive on this point. He asked him to advertise *The history of Mansfield* on the covers of two successive issues of *The Gentleman's Magazine*, and to 'give me your advice respecting advertising, &c'.[98] In a later letter he repeated this instruction, adding that Nichols should phrase the advertisement 'according to the Copy sent or any other form or alteration you think proper'.[99] He continued:

Please also to advertise it *once* in a London paper, likely to promote the sale. And *once* more in any other London paper you think likely to answer the purpose.

In 1808, Harrod was again corresponding with Nichols on this subject.[100]

Please to advertise the History of Harboro' on the outside Cover of your next Gent. Mag. for May, after what Flourish your nature will.

All of this was designed to gain access to the national advertising and distribution system based in London, and only a London bookseller could make it possible.

Even a London bookseller, however, was no guarantee of nationwide sales. Thomas Hervey's *The writer's time redeemed* was published by subscription in 1779, with this imprint:

Kendal: Printed by W. Pennington, and sold by J. Smith, Bradford; J. Matthews, No. 18 in the Strand, and Alexander Hogg, in Pater-noster-Row, London.

John Smith in Bradford, and Matthews and Hogg in London, were merely agents, and, in the case of the Londoners, not particularly successful ones. In fact very few copies were subscribed for south of the Trent (see Appendix V); most of them were taken in Cambridge, where the author may have been known, although he appears not to have been a member of the University.

It is interesting to compare this with Elisha Coles's *Practical discourse of God's sovereignty*, published in 1776:

Bath: Printed and sold by W. Gye; also by S. Hazard, Printer and Bookseller, in King's-Head-Square; and by J. Matthews, Booksellers, No. 18, in the Strand, London. 1776.

Coles was a seventeenth-century Puritan, who had been intruded into both Magdalen College and Magdalen Hall in Oxford during the interregnum; this work was first published in 1673.[101] The important feature of the 1776 edition was not Coles's own text but the 'Recommendatory Preface', mentioned on the title-page, which had been written by William Romaine. Romaine was chaplain to the Countess of Huntingdon, although he stayed within the establishment; in 1776 he held the living of St Andrew-by-the-Wardrobe and St Anne, Blackfriars, and did not break with Lady Huntingdon until she left the Church of England in 1781.[102] He was an influential and popular preacher, and clearly a book recommended by him had a large potential market. Because, however, the market was somewhat specialised, it was published by subscription, and the subscription list is indeed unusual (see Appendix VI). Bath itself provided 305 subscriptions, but 200 of these were from three people: John Lloyd, Esq., who took 100, and Hazard himself and a Mr Barlow, who took 50 each. Of the 200 copies subscribed for in London, 100 each went to Thomas Hunter of Blackfriars, and to Matthews the bookseller. Matthews was here playing his part as wholesaler; Hunter was presumably an acquaintance of Romaine's, and distributing the books for religious reasons, for there is no record of him in the book trade.

In all 976 copies were subscribed for, by 225 subscribers; of these 225, seven are listed without a place of residence, and of those seven, three, including two clergymen, took 100 copies, and one took 50. Thus there were 623 copies subscribed for whose geographical location can be plotted. Except for the 200 copies sent to London, and one sent to Cornwall, all of them were purchased in a small area around Bath itself, extending no further north than Hereford, no further south than Tiverton. The difference between this book and Hervey's is marked, nevertheless, for the 200 copies sent to London, especially Matthews's 100, show that there was an intention to market the book nationally, and that direct subscriptions were in fact a fairly local affair, for customers elsewhere had subscribed through Matthews.

It was, however, possible to organise a very wide distribution of a country book through subscription publication. *A short and plain exposition of the Old Testament* was edited for the press by Robert Gentleman after the death of its author, Job Orton. Orton was a native of Shrewsbury; after an education at the Grammar School there, and at the Warrington and Northampton Academies, followed by two years as a tutor at the latter, he returned to his home town as a Presbyterian minister in 1741. He resigned his ministry in 1765, for health reasons, and eventually went to live at Kidderminster, where he attached himself to the congregation of Robert Gentleman, the dissenting minister in the town. Although he no longer exercised a ministry himself, he was, through his writing and his eloquent preaching, one of the best-known dissenters in the country.[103]

He died in 1783, and in January 1787 proposals were issued for *A short and plain exposition*. The book was of country origin, for the proposals came from Joshua and William Eddowes of Shrewsbury; five London firms were, however, named as agents: James Buckland, Charles Dilly, Joseph Johnson, Thomas Longman, and G. and T. Wilkie.[104] It was published in six volumes between 1788 and 1791.

The first volume contains a list of 588 subscribers who took 646 copies; only one subscriber took as many as ten copies, and most were single copies taken by private individuals. Of the London booksellers who had been named in the prospectus, all except Wilkie were in the imprint:

Shrewsbury: Printed and sold by J. and W. Eddowes. Sold also by T. Longman, and J. Buckland, Paternoster Row; C. Dilly, in the Poultry; and J. Johnson, St. Paul's Church Yard, London. MDCCLXXXVIII.

Orton had a national reputation among the dissenters, and his book was very widely sold (see Appendix VII). There was a concentration of subscribers in his own area, the west midlands, especially in the area bounded by Shrewsbury, Birmingham, and Worcester, but the book also sold well in the east midlands, the west country, East Anglia, and along the southern end of the Yorkshire–Lancashire border; there was a respectable scattering of copies sold in Wales, and even the south midlands, London, and the south-east, traditionally infertile ground for dissent, took a few copies. It ought to be added that 169 of the 646 copies went to subscribers whose place of residence is not recorded. This example shows how widely a provincial book could be disseminated if it had the right London distributors, was widely advertised, and, above all, was of general interest. It is significant that this is a work by a dissenter, and thus not confined by the Anglican tradition of publication in London, Oxford and Cambridge. We may, however, doubt the role the Eddowes brothers played in this; they printed and issued the book, but the marketing was so successful because of their excellent choice of London publishers.

Provincial publishing was very restricted both in scale and in scope. A few provincial books achieved financial success and *succès d'estime* but they were a tiny minority. Far more were purely local publications, or local publications which had a London distributor through whom it was hoped, often in vain, that a wider audience would be attracted. The whole structure of the trade had evolved to take books from London to the provinces, not in the opposite direction. This one-way flow of books is strikingly illustrated by the exception who proves the rule, William Eyres of Warrington in Cheshire.

Eyres inherited his business from his father, John, in 1756.[105] At that time he might have supposed that he was taking over a normally prosperous provincial bookselling and printing business in a flourishing market town. Warrington was a place of some importance; it was on the main road to the north-west of England, it was the first bridging point on the river Mersey, and it was a significant commercial centre for the locality.[106] John Eyres had started his business there in 1731, but confined himself to jobbing work. His son, however, a little more adventurous, began to issue a newspaper, *Eyres Weekly Journal*, which first appeared in March 1756. The pattern was still normal; but the situation changed eighteen months later when Warrington Academy opened its doors.

Warrington was perhaps the most distinguished of all the nonconformist academies; within five years, its tutors included John Aikin, Joseph Priestley, and John Seddon, and in later years Gilbert Wakefield and John Enfield taught there.[107] Eyres took full advantage of the opportunity which had been so fortuitously offered to him. In 1760 he produced just two books, the first ever recorded from the family press. One had twenty-eight pages, the other had four.[108] His next book was Priestley's *A course of lectures on the theory of language and universal grammar* in 1762, a duodecimo of 314 pages.[109] This was not produced without some difficulty, for on 1 May 1762, when Priestley wrote to John Seddon, then the Principal of the Academy, he told him that 'About a fourth part of my Lectures are printed off. Aires is too slow; but he had no help; his boy has left him.'[110] Eyres was still operating on a very small scale, but he rapidly expanded. Between 1760 and 1798 he printed at least 205 books, many of which were written by tutors at the Academy, which remained in Warrington until 1783.[111]

Eyres's publications, because of the presence of an unusually distinguished body of men in the town, are indeed remarkable. He published five books by Priestley, including one very important work, *The history and present state of electricity with original experiments* (1767). He was also responsible for seven books written or translated by Wakefield, ten by Aiken, and sixteen by Enfield. Eyres, moreover, did more than merely print the books: he printed them very well. After his shaky start, he became a skilful printer, the quality of whose work was a matter of contemporary comment. Wakefield was among those who recorded their admiration for it.[112] His reputation was soon attracting authors from outside the Academy. Thomas Pennant, the traveller and zoologist, had a number of friends among the tutors, and it was perhaps through them that he chose Eyres to issue the third edition of his *Tour of Scotland* in 1774, and the fourth edition of his *magnum opus, British zoology*, in 1776.[113] Perhaps the most famous and influential of all the books from Eyres's press was one which he printed in 1777, *The state of the prisons in England and Wales* by John Howard; the author was a close friend of Aiken, who was in fact responsible for seeing the book through the press. Even after the Academy moved from Warrington to Manchester in 1783, Howard, Enfield, and Wakefield each had more than one book printed by Eyres.[114]

It was a remarkable achievement which was possible only because of the existence of the Warrington Academy. Eyres was not the only competent printer outside London, although his work was exceptionally good. He was, however, the only provincial printer with a community of active scholars on his doorstep and no local competition in the trade. Eyres shows us that provincial printers could produce excellent work, but he also illustrates why their publishing activities were so restricted. He was, in fact, like dozens of others, printing books by local authors, most of them clergymen. It is only the quality of the authors which makes Eyres different, and the fact that he seized with both hands the opportunity with which fate had so unexpectedly presented him. To do so he needed a London publisher, and he frequently turned to the radical bookseller Joseph Johnson, who himself issued numerous books by members of the Academy.[115] Johnson was something of an oddity, but he could distribute books as well as his more orthodox colleagues. In 1790, William Frend, a Cambridge Unitarian, told Wakefield that even in that seat of respectable orthodox learning 'We have an Heretical Shelf or two at a Bookseller here by means of Johnson.'[116]

Eyres was unusual in the quality of the books which he published, and the number of important works, which contrast strongly with the unimportant books by insignificant authors which were the normal fare of the provincial printer. A handful of significant books was, however, printed and published by others, and we can identify three classes of serious adult books on which a provincial imprint is not necessarily a value judgement: dissenting theology, medical works, and local histories.

The roots of dissent were most firmly established in the provinces, and this was reinforced by the huge success of the Methodists almost everywhere except London and the south-east, where they failed almost entirely.[117] Whereas Anglican clergymen looked naturally to London and the universities, not least for patronage and preferment, the leading dissenters and Methodists were more provincial in orientation. The Anglican who sought preferment needed to have his books issued by prestigious publishers in London, Oxford, or Cambridge, and to have them nationally circulated. The dissenters were more content with provincial publication, and for a suitably important book like Orton's, national distribution could be arranged. Wesley's first open-air sermon, *Free grace*, was printed in Bristol, where it had been delivered, by Felix Farley in 1739. Farley and another Bristol printer, William Pine, were between them responsible for many of Wesley's subsequent publications.

Medicine was also decentralised. Medical studies at Oxford and Cambridge were little better than a joke, so that most physicians trained in Scotland or on the continent. The Royal Colleges issued their licences to practise, but were otherwise insignificant. A provincial doctor succeeded in his profession by competence, not by patronage, and hence had no need of the prestige and public attention which could be gained from London publication. One of the most important English medical books of the eighteenth century was in fact printed in Birmingham by Myles Swinney. This was William Withering's *Account of the foxglove, and some of its medical properties*, in which the author described for the first time the properties of digitalis, and its use in the treatment of heart disease.[118]

The local historians were the third large group for whom provincial publication was acceptable even for the highest level of work, and for whom it was indeed probably more desirable. One of the earliest histories was Richard Isacke's *Antiquities of the city of Exeter* (1677). This was a London book, without even a named distributor in Exeter:

London: Printed by E. Tyler and R. Holt, for Richard Marriott; sold by George Marriott, at his shop at the sign of the Temple by Inner-Temple Gate, Fleet-Street. 1677.

In 1677 there were still comparatively few booksellers outside London; by 1723, when Isacke's son, Samuel, who had succeeded him as Chamberlain of Exeter, published a revised edition, the city had become an important centre of the trade, and there had been several printers there. The 1723 edition is a provincial book, despite its 'London' imprint:

London: Printed for Edward Score, John March, and Nathaniel Thorne, booksellers in Exon: and Samuel Birt, in Ave-Mary-Lane, London. MDCCXXIII.

Score, March, Thorne, and Birt are the publishers, and the number and order of the names suggests strongly that the initiative for the book came from Exeter, and that the three Exeter booksellers held the greater part of the copyright. The imprint is merely an attempt to give the book a metropolitan appearance.

As with other classes of books, we often find London names in the imprint, even in works of fairly local interest, as in this example:

Sarum: Printed by Chales [*sic*] Hooton, and sold by E. Easton and W. Collins, booksellers in Silver-Street. And also by J. Knapton at the Crown, and T. Astley at the Rose in St. Paul's Church-Yard, London. 1730.

This is the imprint of *A dissertation in vindication of the antiquity of Stone Henge, in answer to the treatises of Mr. Inigo Jones, Dr. Charleton, and all that have written upon that subject*; according to Thomas Hearne, the author of this anonymous book was Stamford Wallis, Vicar of Collingbourne Kingston in Wiltshire.[119] It was a subject of general interest, for it was a contribution to the intermittent controversy about the history and function of Stonehenge,[120] and arrangements were therefore made for distribution in London. On the other hand, it was a book of local interest, for which Wallis had probably been obliged to seek a local publisher; the description of him on the title-page, as 'a Clergyman living in the Neighbourhood of the Famous Monument', suggests that his proximity was his only claim to authority.

Some local histories were even more local than this. Henry Rooke's *A sketch of the ancient and present state of Sherwood Forest*, for example, was printed at the author's expense, probably in a tiny edition, for the imprint gives no distributor:

Nottingham: Printed by S. Tupman. M, DCC, XCIX.

The imprint of *A survey of the city of Worcester* by Valentine Green is only a little less reticent:

Worcester: Printed by J. Butler for S. Gamidge, at Prior's Head. MDCCLXIV.

In 1764 Green was an apprentice in Worcester, but a year later he moved to London, where he achieved a great reputation as a mezzotint engraver.[121] In 1796 he published a revised, indeed virtually rewritten, edition of this book, as *The history and antiquities of the city and suburbs of Worcester*. The book, published by subscription and dedicated to George III, who had visited Worcester in 1788 during the holiday which was intended to restore his rapidly failing health,[122] was distributed by some of the leading members of the trade:

London: Printed for the author by W. Bulmer and co. and sold by G. Nichol, Bookseller to His Majesty, Edwards, White, Cadell, Payne, Robson, Stockdale, Leigh and Sotheby, Egerton, Hookham and Carpenter, Shepperson and Reynolds; and in Worcester, by Smart, Tymbs, Holl, Andrews and Gamidge, booksellers. MDCCXCVI.

By that time, Green, a famous artist, had outgrown provincial publication.

The 1796 edition of Green's book was very different from its predecessor. It was in two handsome quarto volumes, elegantly printed, and with many plates of considerable artistic merit. It is a reminder that the eighteenth century was the great age of the county history, and that these rank among the finest and most useful products of the provincial printers. Not all of them were provincial books, but a high proportion was, perhaps as many as 60%.[123] Most of the large-scale county histories were published by subscription, or at the author's expense. This was true, for example, of Edward Hasted's *History and topographical survey of the county of Kent* (Canterbury, Printed for the author, by Simmons and Kirkby. MDCCLXXVIII), and of William Hutchinson's *History of the county of Cumberland* (Carlisle, 2 vols., 1794). It was even true of some smaller works, such as Edmund Carter's *History of the county of Cambridge* (Cambridge: Printed for the author; and sold by T. James, printer, and R. Matthews, bookseller in Cambridge. 1753). Some imprints are less explicit, but almost certainly conceal authorial publication; examples are John Lodge's *Introductory sketches towards a topographical history of the county of Hereford* (Kington: Printed and sold by J. Barrel; sold also by J. Allen, Hereford; J. Barrow and F. Harris, Leominster; and J. Robinson, Paternoster-Row, London. M.DCC.XCIII.), and Peter Muilman's *New and complete history of Essex* (Chelmsford: Printed and sold by Lionel Hassall. MDCCLXIX.).

Even a cursory survey of provincial publishing demonstrates the success of the London trade in retaining their control over the lucrative business of providing books to satisfy the demands of an ever-growing market. The provincial printers, despite having a few important titles to their credit, were left with little more than the scraps from the London table. The English book trade was unshakeably metropolitan in its organisation, and the provincial printers had to look elsewhere than book printing for their work. They adapted well. The provincial printers existed to fill gaps in the market, where demand was either so local or, as with the chapbooks, so great that the London houses were either unwilling to undertake the work or unable to cope with it. The provincial printer of the eighteenth century was a jobbing printer; some also printed newspapers, chapbooks, ballads, almanacs, and books, but it was the endless flow of handbills, tickets, and catalogues which occupied most of the time of most of the printers of provincial England.

Conclusion

In 1700 as in 1800 England was engaged in a long and bitter war with France; William III fought to defend a revolution, William Pitt fought to suppress one. Pitt's greatest enemy described his opponents in terms of contempt as a nation of shopkeepers, but they accepted the description with pride. The transformation of the retail trades was less dramatic than that of the productive industries, but no less profound. In 1800, it was still incomplete, and was to be so until the modern pattern of distribution and sales was established by the building of the railways. For most of the eighteenth century, England's economy retained its traditional regional pattern, and only slowly was the country's economic geography changed by the imperatives of mass-production. Of that change the book trade was a harbinger. While most goods were still consumed in the locality of their production, the book trade historically dealt in products manufactured in bulk and distributed widely.

By the standards of 1700, the book trade was a large-scale mass-production industry; in 1800 it was not, but the booksellers had by then unwittingly pioneered the development of nationwide distribution. The social, political, and cultural influence of this achievement was out of all proportion to its economic scale. Although regional cultures survived, a uniform national culture was superimposed upon them through the uniformity of the printed word. The London newspapers, distributed by the Post Office, became a national medium of information, opinion, and advertising. Their advertising function was of exceptional value to the booksellers. The growth of a literate middle class, and the spread of literacy far down the social scale, created a market of unprecedented size. An elaborate system of distribution was developed which made the same book as readily available in Penzance or Carlisle as it was in Paternoster Row or Pall Mall.

The provincial book trade was dominated by the newspaper proprietors, wealthy men commanding power and respect in their communities. It was they who established the networks of newsagents and newsmen who took books into the towns and villages of provincial

England, and were the final link in the chain between writer and reader. What they sold was a product which conveyed metropolitan ideas. The dominance of the metropolis had never been so obvious as it was by the end of the eighteenth century, and in that fact lay the seeds of the future. In 1700, London ran the country; by 1800, it was obvious that London ran the country. The distinction is crucial, for the blatant display of metropolitan domination in the printed word reached its highest point of development in those very decades when the balance of economic power was shifting northwards and into the cities. The wide availability of newspapers and books had created an unprecedented degree of political awareness in the provinces, supported on a firm base of metropolitan culture. Imitation gave way to competition; the new masters of the economy began to challenge the old masters of the established order. New ideas, whether expressed in the strident sentences of Tom Paine or the more philosophic paragraphs of Adam Smith, penetrated the consciousness of provincial England. The radicalisation of the provincial press at the end of the century, a subject deserving of a book to itself, was the first expression of revolt. While Pitt suppressed the opposition, a few provincial newspaper owners exploited the independence of the distribution system from government control through the Post Office to circulate in the country ideas which in London were strangled at birth. The book trade, from its humble origins in the ill-equipped offices of the first provincial printers, had brought forth a most unexpected progeny. In 1800, the age of the provinces was about to begin.

APPENDIX I
Ellen Feepound's Book Stock

Extract from: Staffordshire R.O. Q/5B 1776, Debtors Trans. 1776.
The transcript is confined to the list of books in Ellen Feepound's shop; it was made as part of the bankruptcy proceedings against her on 13 June 1776.

An account of which Books remain unsold of my Printed Catalogue –

N° 2   The Life of our Blessed Saviour
                    Folio
   3   A commentary on the Book of Leviticus
   4   Divine Meditations on the 29th Psalm
   5   Bishop Jewel's Reply to Harding
   6   Bishop Jewel's Defence of the Apology of the Church
   8   A Treatise of the 5th Council held at Constantinople
   9   The Holy Court
  11   Sheppard's Practical Counsellor
  12   Cromwell's Acts
                  Quarto and Octavo &c.
  14   The History of Europe
  16   The Illiads of Homer &c.
  18   The Considerations of Drexellus in Eternity &c.
  19   The Devilfulness of Mans heart &c.
  20   Romish Doctrines not from the Beginning &c.
  21   Seven Treatises guiding to true Happiness
  22   Tenieurs Melody of the Heart
  23   Colling's Vindication of a Gospel Ministry
  24   A Sermon at the Funeral of Sir Edmondbury Godfrey &c.
  25   A Defence of the Ecclesiastical Polity
  26   A Reproof of the Rehearsal
  27   An Answer to the Dissenters Plea of Separation
  29   Blackwell's Discourses on the right Method of Preaching
  30   Brooksby's History of the Government of the Primitive Church
  31   Stevenson's Sacred History
  32   Templar's Treatise on Worship
  33   Wall's History of Infant Baptism
  35   Spiritual Communion Recommended
  36   The Exemplary Life of James Bonnell Esq[r]
  37   Fleetwood's Essay on Miracles
  39   Christian Eloquence in Theory and Practice

41 The whole Duty of a Christian &c.
50 A Method for Private Devotion
51 Corbett's discourse on Prayer &c.
53 An Essay upon Friendship &c.
54 Pagis on Separation from the Church &c.
56 The devout Christmas Companion
57 Edward on Preaching 2 Vol:
58 Whitby on Christian Faith
59 The Christian Religion Explained &c.
60 A Serious Answer to D.ʳ Trapp &c.
61 A Plain Exposition of Several Chapters of Proverbs
62 M.ʳ Hobbes's Leviathan Observed, Censured, &c.
63 An Essay for a Review of the Book of Common Prayer
64 A Plausible Argument of a Romish Priest Answered
65 Taylors Rule & Exercises of Holy Living &c.
66 An Essay in Defence of the Female Sex &c.
67 Bennets Review on the Case of Liturgies &c.
69 The Christian Sacrifice &c.
70 The Friendly debate of a Conformist & Nonconformist &c.
72 The Psalm Singers Choice Companion
73 Denham's Version of the Psalms &c.
74 Darney's Collection of Hymns &c.
75 A Version of the Psalms &c.
79 The Humourist &c.
81 A Vindication of the Parliament &c.
82 The Madness of Disaffection & Treason &c.
83 Essays of Michael Signeur de Montaigne &c.
84 Essays on Peace and War
86 Browns Roman History
92 Military Discipline &c.
93 Houl's Common Accidence &c.
94 Bailey's English & Latin Exercises &c.
95 Clarks Introduction to the making of Latin
97 Willymott's Collection of Sentences
98 Shaw's new Grammar for Classick Writers
99 Lock's Esop Fables in English & Latin
101 Walkers Treatise of English Particles
104 Wingates Arithmetick
108 A Manual of Prayer &c.
109 Animadversions of Greek & Latin Historians
110 Collins's Gauger &c.
111 Truth brought to light, &c.
112 Rymer's Tragedies, &c.
113 Essays on the Balance of Power
114 A Letter concerning Enthusiasm &c.
115 The Penetential Discipline of the Primitive Church

116 Cave's Primitive Christianity
117 The Jews Sabbath Antiquated & Lord's Day Justified
118 The Psalter of David &c.
119 Bernard's Christian Conscience &c.
120 Brief Notes on M.ʳ Roger's Catechism &c.
121 Time and the end of Time &c.
122 Caley's Glimpse of Eternity &c.
123 Attorneys Pocket Companion
124 Hernes's Law of Conveyances &c.
125 Law of Bastardy &c.
126 Young Clerks Guide &c.
127 A Collection of Statutes on Laws of Excise
128 Instructor Clericalis 2 Vol:
129 A Treatise on Fines &c.
130 The Gentlemans Assistant and Tradesmans Lawyer
131 Jacobs Land Stewards Assistant
132 A Preparative to Pleading
133 Tryals [*illegible*], Or the Law of Juries by Msr.[?] Pring [?] &c.
134 The Law of Trespasses
135 The Law against Bankrupts
136 The Laws against Immorality & Prophaneness
137 The Law of Trover and Conversion
138 The Mysteries of Clerkship Explained
139 The Method of Pleading by Rules & President
140 The Office & Authority of a Justice of Peace
141 A Discourse on Grants & Resumptions
142 A Treatise on Copyhold Estates
143 The Impartial Lawyer
144 A Complete Guide for Justices of Peace
145 The Complete Arbitrator
146 The Office of an Attorney
147 The Entring Clerks Introduction
148 Styles's Practical Register
149 The Clerks Tutor in Chancery
150 The Course of Proceedings in High Court of Chancery
151 An Essay for the Regulation of the Law
152 Law Quibbles
153 Officium Clerici Pacis, Indictments, Informations &c.
154 The Law concerning Tryals
156 The Method of keeping Country Courts &c.
158 The Parsons Counsellor, with the Law of Tythes
159 Spelman's Tracts for Tythes
160 An Introduction to the Study and Practice of the Law
161 The Law of Executions
163 Natura Brevium, Corrected and Revised
164 Kilburn's Presidents relating to the Office of a Justice

165 Wingate's Abridgment of the Statutes
166 Washington's Abridgment of the Statutes
167 The Complete Sheriff
169 Browns Collection of Presidents for Fines &c.
170 The Country Parsons Companion
171 The Rights of the Christian Church
172 Nelsons Office of a Justice of Peace
173 The Attorney's Pocket Companion in two Parts
174 Barrows Psalm Singers Companion
175 Fruits of Retirement &c.
176 A Guide to Practisers of the Law, in two parts
178 A Treatise on Fines, &c.
179 The present state of England
180 The Solicitor &c.
183 A Physical Treatise grounded on Experience
184 A Treatise on Wounds
185 A new discovery of the Scurvey &c.
186 A Treatise of the Ricketts, &c.
187 The Sea Chirurgeon &c.
188 Cook's Supplement to the Marrow of Chirurgery
189 A Defence of Scarborough Spaw &c.
190 Shipton's Pharmocopeia &c.
191 Fuller's Pharmocopeia &c.
194 Gerardi Blasiae Observata Anatomica &c.
195 Keil's Anatomy of Human Body Abridg'd &c.
196 The Experienced Chirurgeon, &c.
197 Harvey's Anatomical Exercises, &c.
198 Pharmacopeia Collegii Regalis Londini &c.

And an account of what Books remain unsold that were not in my Printed
Catalogue Nor Number'd on the Backs
Folio
A large Second Hand Bible Old Print
Statutes at Large Vol: 1st
Nelson's Abridgment of the Law 3 Vol:
Octavo &c.
Lilly's Practical Register 2 Vol:
Style's Practical Register
Compleat Attorney
Washington's Abridgment of the Statutes 2 Vol:
Complete Chancery Practiser 2 Vols.
Praxis Curiae Cancellar: 3 Vol:
Praxis Almae 2 Vol:
Arcana Clericalis, Or The Mysteries of Clerkship Exp.
Wingate's Abridgment of the Statutes
A Testament Second Hand Old Print

Ellen Feepound's Book Stock

A Common Prayer Book with New Testament Second Hand
Courayers defence of English Ordinations 3 Vol:
Mollineux's Fruits of Retirement
More on Episcopacy
Church Censures
The Spinner Condemned of Himself
Answer to the Touchstone of the Reformed Gospel
A Letter from M.ʳ Smith to D.ʳ Hammond & Answer
The Church Catechism Explained
The Reasonable Communicant
A Companion to the Altar
Russel's Seven Sermons
The Life of God in the Soul of Men
The Countess of Moretons Daily Exercise
And about 30 Small old Books in Divinity History Physick & Law
and about 140 Books for Scholars in English and Latin &c.
and also about 30 Books in the Circulating Library

There is also some Quills and Pens, Pensils, Inkhorns & Ink
Some Writing Paper and other Paper Some New Paper for Hangings and old
    Paper Hangings Some Maps Pictures & Pack Thread
Some Historys Carols and Garlands &c.
7 Papers of Holmans Ink Powder
Some Galls and some Salt Petre
1 Bottle of Lees Excellent Water for the Toothach
1 Bottle of Schwanbers Liquid Shell for the Stone & Gravel
And some Cannisters with some other trifling Things.

William Seale's Paper Stock

Extract from: Oxford University Archives. Chancellor's Court Inventories, Vol. R–S, Hyp./B/18.

The transcript is of the paper stock only, from an inventory prepared for probate on 23 April 1719.

Paper of the New-Stock

2 Reams of Imperial	8–11–0
2 Reams of Royal	4–10–0
2 Reams of best Demy	2–10–6
2 Reams of Demy	2–0–0
1 Ream of Marble	1–5–0
2 Reams of Gilt large 4to	0–18–0
2 Reams of 2^d Fool's-Cap	2–4–0
6 Reams of Superfine Fool's-Cap	4–1–0
Ruling 3 reams of 2^d Fool's-Cap	0–3–0
10 Reams of Fine King's Arms	5–8–0
1 Ream of Superfine-Royal	3–3–0
3 Reams of Kings-Arms	1–7–0
2 Reams more of Superfine Fool's-cap	1–7–0

In the Old Stock

11 Reams of City-Arms	4–14–0
30 Reams of Pro Patria	15–10–6
1 Ream of Superfine Royal	3–3–0
1 Ream of Royal	2–5–0
1 Ream of a smaller Royal	1–16–0
2 Reams of best Demy	2–10–6
8 Reams of Cardinal's Arms	3–11–0
3 Reams of Cardinal's Arms	1–12–6
8 Reams of Superfine Amst. Arms	4–6–6
2 Reams of Horn-Pott	0–13–6
2 Reams of Fine Card. Arms	2–0–6
¾ of a Ream Imperial	3–4–0
2 Parcels of Gilt and Coloured Paper	0–4–0
½ Ream of best Demy	0–12–6
¾ of a Ream more, of best Demy	0–19–0
18 Quires of Marble-Paper	1–3–6
12 Quires of the best Demy	0–13–6

William Seale's Paper Stock

5 Quires of Royal	0–11–6
Several old Parcels of Paper	0–17–0
15 Quires of large Brown-Cap	0–4–0
Several Parcels of Gilt Paper	1–7–0
Several Parcels of loose Paper	1–2–6
Paper-Books of several Sizes	2–2–0

John Cheney's Printing Equipment

Transcript of: a list of type and equipment in John Cheney and Sons Ltd., Banbury. Archives.

This document, transcribed in full, is in the hand of John Cheney. It is probably to be dated 1788, when Cheney moved to his new premises in Red Lion Street, Banbury. The move was complete by 12 June 1788, when Cheney issued a handbill to advertise his new address.

			£	s	d
Six lines Pica	62½ lb	1 Case at 1/–	3	2	6
Canon	116	3 do	5	16	0
Old English Black	61	2 do	3	2	0
2 lines G.ᵗ Primer	87	3 do	4	7	0
2 lines English	90	3 do	4	10	0
Double Pica	111	4 do	5	11	0
Great Primer (new)	94	4 do	4	14	0
Old English	137	5 do	6	17	0
Natt. English	116½	6 do	5	16	6
Pica on English	136	6 do	6	16	0
English on Pica	156	4 do	7	10	0
New Pica	171	6 do at 1/2ᵈ	9	19	6
Pica 3 nicks	232	7 do 1/–	11	12	0
Old Pica	204	9 do 4ᵈ	3	8	0
Small Pica	156	6 do	7	16	0
Long Primmer	163	10 do 1/–	8	3	0
Dᵒ	68		3	8	0
Brevier	62	4 do	3	2	0
Odd Letter	57		2	17	0
Two line fancy	16	1 do at 2/–	1	12	0
Quadrats &c.	140		7	0	0
Old Metal	140	16	3	10	0
Dᵒ	15	Old Metal 175 lb	3	10	0
	2591				
Dᵒ	20				

86 cases at 4/–	17	4	0
Stands &c.	5	0	0
11 Chases	4	0	0
5 Gallies & 2 slices &c.	1	0	0
Brass rules & other brass ornaments	5	0	0
Furniture, Pictures &c.	20	0	0
2 Presses	25	0	0
	176	7	6

The Universal British Directory

For a discussion of the *Universal British Directory*, and the evidence afforded by it, see pp. 29–30, above. There follows an alphabetical list of towns in England, more than twenty miles from London, in which members of the book trade are recorded in *UBD*.

1	Abingdon	34	Bilston
2	Alcester	35	Birmingham
3	Alnwick	36	Bishop's Castle
4	Alresford	37	Bishop's Stortford
5	Alton	38	Blackburn
6	Ampthill	39	Blandford Forum
7	Andover	40	Bodmin
8	Appleby	41	Bolsover
9	Arundel	42	Bolton
10	Ashbourne	43	Boston
11	Ashburton	44	Boxford
12	Ashby-de-la-Zouche	45	Brackley
13	Ashford	46	Bradford
14	Atherstone	47	Brentwood
15	Axminster	48	Bridgewater
16	Aylesbury	49	Bridlington
17	Banbury	50	Bridport
18	Barnard Castle	51	Brighton
19	Barnsley	52	Bristol
20	Barnstaple	53	Brompton
21	Barton-on-Humber	54	Bromsgrove
22	Basingstoke	55	Buckingham
23	Bath	56	Bungay
24	Battle	57	Burford
25	Bawtry	58	Burnley
26	Beccles	59	Burwash
27	Bedford	60	Bury
28	Berkhempstead	61	Bury St Edmunds
29	Berwick-upon-Tweed	62	Buxton
30	Beverley	63	Calne
31	Bewdley	64	Cambridge
32	Bideford	65	Canterbury
33	Biggleswade	66	Carlisle

67	Castor	113	Falmouth
68	Cerne	114	Faversham
69	Chatham	115	Frome
70	Chelmsford	116	Gainsborough
71	Cheltenham Spa	117	Garstang
72	Chertsey	118	Gateshead
73	Chesham	119	Glamford Briggs
74	Chester	120	Glastonbury
75	Chesterfield	121	Gloucester
76	Chichester	122	Godalming
77	Chippenham	123	Gosport
78	Chipping Norton	124	Grantham
79	Chorley	125	Gravesend
80	Cirencester	126	Great Yarmouth
81	Cockermouth	127	Guildford
82	Colchester	128	Hadleigh
83	Colne	129	Halesworth
84	Congleton	130	Halifax
85	Coventry	131	Hanley
86	Cowes	132	Harlow
87	Cranbrook	133	Haslingden
88	Crewkerne	134	Hastings
89	Darlington	135	Havant
90	Dartmouth	136	Hawkshead
91	Daventry	137	Helston
92	Deal	138	Hemel Hempstead
93	Derby	139	Henley-on-Thames
94	Devizes	140	Hereford
95	Doncaster	141	Hertford
96	Dorchester	142	High Wycombe
97	Dorking	143	Hinkley
98	Dover	144	Hitchin
99	Downham	145	Holt
100	Driffield	146	Honiton
101	Dudley	147	Horncastle
102	Dunmow	148	Horsham
103	Dunstable	149	Howden
104	Durham	150	Huddersfield
105	East Dereham	151	Hull
106	East Grinstead	152	Huntingdon
107	Ellesmere	153	Hythe
108	Ely	154	Ilminster
109	Emsworth	155	Ipswich
110	Eton	156	Keighley
111	Evesham	157	Kendal
112	Exeter	158	Keswick

159	Kettering	205	Northwich
160	Kidderminster	206	Norwich
161	King's Lynn	207	Nottingham
162	Kirkham	208	Nuneaton
163	Knaresborough	209	Oakham
164	Knutsford	210	Oakingham
165	Lancaster	211	Ormskirk
166	Launceston	212	Oswestry
167	Lavenham	213	Oxford
168	Leeds	214	Penrith
169	Leek	215	Penryn
170	Leicester	216	Penzance
171	Leominster	217	Pershore
172	Lewes	218	Peterborough
173	Lichfield	219	Petworth
174	Lincoln	220	Plymouth
175	Liverpool	221	Plymouth Dock (Devonport)
176	Loughborough	222	Pocklington
177	Louth	223	Pontefract
178	Ludlow	224	Poole
179	Macclesfield	225	Portsea
180	Maidenhead	226	Portsmouth
181	Maidstone	227	Prescot
182	Maldon	228	Preston
183	Manchester	229	Reading
184	Mansfield	230	Redruth
185	Margate	231	Retford
186	Market Harborough	232	Ripon
187	Marlborough	233	Rochdale
188	Marlow	234	Rochester
189	Melton Mowbray	235	Romsey
190	Middlewich	236	Rotherham
191	Midhurst	237	Royston
192	Moretonhampstead	238	Rugby
193	Morpeth	239	Rugeley
194	Nantwich	240	Rye
195	Newark	241	St Albans
196	Newbury	242	St Austell
197	Newcastle-under-Lyme	243	St Ives
198	Newcastle-upon-Tyne	244	St Neots
199	Newmarket	245	Salisbury
200	Newport, I.O.W.	246	Sandwich
201	Newport, Salop	247	Scarborough
202	Newport Pagnell	248	Settle
203	Northallerton	249	Shaftesbury
204	Northampton	250	Sheffield

251	Shepton Mallett	284	Ulverston
252	Sherborne	285	Uttoxeter
253	Shrewsbury	286	Wakefield
254	Sleaford	287	Wallingford
255	Snaith	288	Walsall
256	Southam	289	Walsham
257	Southampton	290	Wantage
258	South Molton	291	Ware
259	Southwell	292	Warminster
260	Spalding	293	Warrington
261	Stafford	294	Warwick
262	Stamford	295	Wellingborough
263	Stockport	296	Wellington
264	Stockton-on-Tees	297	Wells
265	Stonehouse	298	Weymouth
266	Stourbridge	299	Whitby
267	Stowmarket	300	Whitchurch
268	Stratford-upon-Avon	301	Whitehaven
269	Sudbury	302	Wigan
270	Sunderland	303	Wimbourne Minster
271	Swaffham	304	Winchester
272	Swinton	305	Windsor
273	Tamworth	306	Winster
274	Taunton	307	Wirksworth
275	Tavistock	308	Witham
276	Tenterden	309	Wolverhampton
277	Tewkesbury	310	Woodbridge
278	Thaxted	311	Woodstock
279	Thirsk	312	Wootton-under-Edge
280	Tiverton	313	Worcester
281	Torrington	314	Workington
282	Trowbridge	315	Yeovil
283	Truro	316	York

APPENDIX V

Subscribers to Thomas Hervey's
The Writer's Time Redeemed

The book was published at Kendal in 1779. For a discussion, see p. 113, above.

Number of subscribers	Places
1	Blackburn; Bootle; Broughton (Lincs.); Crossthwaite; Ireleth; Hawkshead; Hutton; Lindale; London; Lupton; Stokesley; Newark; North Muskham; Nottingham; Orston; Oxford; Pennington; Sawley; Stockport; Wakefield; Whicham
2–5	Cartmel; Dalton-in-Furness; Heckmondwyke; Leeds; Liverpool; Rotherham; Ulpha; Ulverston; Witherslack
6–10	Cambridge; Lancaster; Levenshulme; Preston
11–15	NONE
16–20	Kendal

Subscribers to Elisha Coles's *Practical Discourse*

The book was published at Bath in 1776. For a discussion, see pp. 113–14, above.

Number of subscribers	Places
1	Compton Dander; Hereford; Hullalvington; St Agnes; Tiverton; Upton
2–5	Bradford-on-Avon; Malmesbury; Marshfield; Melksham; Tetbury
6–10	Chipping Sodbury; Dursley; Trowbridge
11–15	Beckington; Rode
16–30	NONE
31–50	Frome
51–199	NONE
200	London
305	Bath

Subscribers to Job Orton's *Short and Plain Exposition*

The book was published at Shrewsbury and London, in six volumes, between 1788 and 1791. For a discussion, see pp. 114–15, above.

Region	1	2–5	6–10	11–15	16–20	21–30	31–50
				Number of subscribers			
London & SE*	15	6	0	0	0	0	1
West Midlands*	20	12	5	1	0	0	2
East Midlands*	15	3	0	0	0	0	0
South Midlands*	4	6	2	0	0	0	0
E. Anglia/Lincs*	8	3	1	0	0	0	0
West Riding	2	7	1	1	0	0	0
North East*	4	1	0	0	0	0	0
Lancs/Cheshire	5	6	2	0	0	0	0
North West*	1	0	0	0	0	0	0
West*	14	8	1	0	0	1	0
Wales	17	5	0	0	0	0	0

* These regions are defined as follows:

London & SE	London; Berkshire; Buckinghamshire; Hampshire; Hertfordshire; Kent; Middlesex; Oxfordshire; Surrey; Sussex
West Midlands	Gloucestershire; Shropshire; Staffordshire; Warwickshire; Worcestershire
East Midlands	Derbyshire; Leicestershire; Nottinghamshire; Rutland
South Midlands	Bedfordshire; Huntingdonshire; Northamptonshire
E. Anglia/Lincs	Cambridgeshire; Essex; Lincolnshire; Norfolk; Suffolk
North East	Durham; Northumberland; Yorkshire (East and North Ridings)
North West	Cumberland; Westmoreland
West	Cornwall; Devon; Dorset; Wiltshire

Notes

CHAPTER 1. LONDON AND THE COUNTRY

1. Raymond Astbury. The renewal of the Licensing Act in 1693 and its lapse in 1695. *The Library*, 5th ser., 33 (1978), pp. 296–322. Timothy Crist. Government control of the press after the expiration of the Printing Act in 1679. *Publishing History*, 5 (1979), pp. 49–77.

2. R. Stewart-Brown. The stationers, booksellers and printers of Chester to about 1800. *Transactions of the Historic Society of Lancashire and Cheshire*, 83 (1931), p. 107.

3. R. B. McKerrow. *A dictionary of the printers and booksellers in England, Scotland and Ireland, and of foreign printers of English books 1555–1640*. London, 1910, p. 143; and the imprint of *STC* 23697.

4. C. J. Hunt. *The book trade in Northumberland and Durham to 1860*. Newcastle-upon-Tyne, 1975, p. 26.

5. C. W. Chilton. Inventory of a provincial bookseller's stock in 1644. *The Library*, 6th ser., 1 (1979), pp. 126–43. A similar shop existed, for example, at Banbury in Oxfordshire; see the *DNB* article on William Whately.

6. E. A. Clough. *A short-title catalogue, arranged geographically, of books printed and distributed . . . in the English provincial towns and in Scotland and Ireland up to and including the year 1700*. London, 1969.

7. John Latimer. *The annals of Bristol in the eighteenth century*. Bristol, 1893, pp. 48–49.

8. R. M. Wiles. *Freshest advices. Early provincial newspapers in England*. Columbus, Ohio, 1965, pp. 14–15, 383.

9. See below, Chapter 2, pp. 12–31.

10. R. C. Bald. Early copyright litigation and its bibliographical interest. *PBSA*, 36 (1940), pp. 81–96. John Feather. The book trade in politics: the making of the Copyright Act of 1710. *Publishing History*, 8 (1980), pp. 19–44.

11. The term was used by the bookseller John Dunton, in *A voyage round the world*. London, 3 vols., 1691, vol. 2, p. 177. For the operation of the system, see Norma Hodgson and Cyprian Blagden. *The notebook of Thomas Bennet and Henry Clements (1686–1719)*. Oxford (Oxford Bibliographical Society, new ser., 6), 1956, pp. 67–70; and Graham Pollard. The English market for printed books. *Publishing History*, 4 (1978), pp. 7–48, esp. pp. 26–27.

12. Hodgson and Blagden, *op. cit.*, p. 84.

Notes to pp. 3–7

13. Cyprian Blagden. Booksellers' trade sales 1718–1768. *The Library*, 5th ser., 5 (1950–51), pp. 243–57. Terry Belanger. Booksellers' trade sales, 1718–1768. *The Library*, 5th ser., 30 (1975), pp. 281–302.
14. Blagden, Booksellers' trade sales, p. 244.
15. *Ibid.*, p. 256. Hodgson and Blagden, *op. cit.*, p. 97.
16. Marjorie Plant. *The English book trade*. London, 3rd ed., 1974, p. 88.
17. Charles Welsh. *A bookseller of the last century*. London, 1885, pp. 19n, 58–59. Albert H. Smith. The printing and publication of the early editions of the novels of Tobias George Smollett. London University Ph.D. thesis, 1975, vol. 2, pp. 34–52.
18. R. A. Austen-Leigh. Joseph Pote of Eton and Bartlet's *Farriery*. *The Library*, 4th ser., 17 (1936–37), pp. 131–54.
19. *Parliamentary History*, vol. 27, cols. 1093, 1097. James J. Barnes. *Free trade in books*. Oxford, 1964, p. 59.
20. Bodleian Library, MS Add. c 89, f. 119*.
21. Smith, *op. cit.*, vol. 2, pp. 344–45.
22. Robert L. Haig. *The Gazetteer 1735–1797*. Carbondale, Ill., 1960, p. 148.
23. Belanger, *op. cit.*, p. 283.
24. Joseph Shaylor. *The fascination of books*. London, 1912, pp. 165–69.
25. The most recent account of this complex subject is Gwyn Walters. The booksellers in 1759 and 1774: the battle for literary property. *The Library*, 5th ser., 29 (1974), pp. 287–311.
26. *Parliamentary History*, vol. 27, cols. 1078–1110.
27. Leonard Jay (ed.). *Letters of the famous 18th century printer John Baskerville of Birmingham*. Birmingham, 1932, p. 9. They subsequently reached an agreement.
28. 12 George II, c. 36. See John Feather. The English book trade and the law, 1695–1799. *Publishing History*, 12 (1982), pp. 57–58.
29. Nor did the Act apply to Berwick-upon-Tweed, a fact which the printers there appear to have exploited. More work is needed on the possibility that books with false imprints were printed in Berwick for illegal import into England. The only such book known to me with a deliberately falsified imprint is the 'fifteenth' (1753) edition of Locke's *Essay concerning human understanding*. The copy in the British library has the imprint 'Berwick, Robert Taylor'; that in the Bodleian has a cancel title-leaf, with the imprint 'Printed in the year M.DCC.LIII'. The place of origin is not mentioned in the cancellans. The date is genuine, however, so the text was in public domain under the 1710 Act.
30. For the background to this bill, and to all the legal issues, see Lyman Ray Patterson. *Copyright in historical perspective*. Nashville, Tenn., 1968, pp. 151–79. See also Walters, *op. cit., passim*.
31. *CJ*, 22, p. 400.
32. The London edition was in 1731. The Dublin edition is dated 'MDCCXXII', but this must be an error for MDCCXXXII.
33. Plomer, *op. cit.*, pp. 153–54.

34. London, 1730; Edinburgh, 1732; Dublin, 1733.
35. *CJ*, 22, p. 412.
36. This, and the other letters discussed here, were printed by Alexander Donaldson. *Some thoughts on the state of literary property*. London, 1764. See also A. S. Collins. *Authorship in the days of Johnson*. London, 1927. Collins points out that their 'authenticity was never challenged'; this is true, but beside the point. What is open to doubt is Donaldson's interpretation, for he was hardly a neutral observer; and Collins, p. 92, unfortunately followed Donaldson without question.
37. The exceptions are Swift's *Works*, and Young's *Works* and *Night thoughts*.
38. They were not, however, as indefensible as has been maintained by Collins, *op. cit.*, *passim*, again influenced by Donaldson. Their point was a nice one, and occupied some of the best legal brains of both kingdoms for two decades before it was finally decided. W. Forbes Gray. Alexander Donaldson and his fight for cheap books. *Juridical Review*, 38 (1926), pp. 180–202.
39. *Parliamentary History*, vol. 27, cols. 1078–1110. Cobbett's account is heavily favourable to the Londoners, and gives far more detailed accounts of their speeches than of those of their opponents.

CHAPTER 2. A CENTURY OF GROWTH

1. Margaret Spufford. *Small books and pleasant histories. Popular fiction and its readership in seventeenth-century England*. London, 1981, pp. 111–28.
2. David Alexander. *Retailing in England during the industrial revolution*. London, 1970, pp. 36–50.
3. Michael Sparke. *A second beacon fired by Scintilla*. London, 1652, pp. 5–6.
4. Imprint of Wing D435. For the markets, see Richard Blome. *Britannia: or a geographical description of the kingdoms of England, Scotland and Ireland*. London, 1673, pp. 44, 120, 139, 175–77, 191.
5. George Birkbeck Hill (ed.). *Boswell's Life of Johnson*, rev. L. F. Powell. Oxford, 6 vols., 1964–71, vol. 1, p. 36. P. B. Freshwater (ed.). *Working papers for an historical directory of the west midlands book trade*. Pt 1, Birmingham, 1975, p. 10.
6. John Feather. John Clay of Daventry. The business of an eighteenth-century stationer. *SB*, 37 (1984), pp. 198–209.
7. Plomer, *op. cit.*, pp. 96–97. Plomer, Bushnell, and Dix, *op. cit.*, p. 70. John Nichols. *Literary anecdotes of the eighteenth century*. London, 9 vols., 1812–15, vol. 3, p. 674.
8. P.R.O. PROB 11/1227/19.
9. Pollard, Market, p. 14.
10. Alexander Rodger. Ward's Shrewsbury stock: an inventory of 1585. *The Library*, 5th ser., 13 (1958), pp. 247–68.

11. Plomer, *op. cit.*, pp. 20–21. Herbert E. Norris. Cirencester booksellers and printers. *NQ*, 11th ser., 11 (1915), p. 141.
12. Feather, John Clay, pp. 199, 209.
13. Plomer, *op. cit.*, p. 270. Giles Hester. *Nevill Simmons, bookseller and publisher*. London, 1893.
14. It has been suggested that he was related to Clement Barksdale, born at Winchcombe, Gloucs., and later Vicar of Naunton and Stow-on-the-Wold (*DNB*), but there is no real evidence. See F. A. Hyett. *Supplement to the Bibliographer's manual of Gloucestershire literature*. Gloucester, 1915, pp. 21–22.
15. Plomer, *op. cit.*, p. 175. Llewlyn C. Lloyd. The book trade in Shropshire. Some account of the stationers, booksellers and printers at work in the county to about 1800. *Transactions of the Shropshire Archaeological Society*, 18 (1934–35), pp. 85–86. A. Crawford and A. P. Jones. The early typography of printed Welsh. *The Library*, 6th ser., 3 (1981), pp. 222–24.
16. Lloyd, *op. cit.*, p. 91. Wiles, *op. cit.*, pp. 16–17, 497–98.
17. J. Ingle Dredge. Devon booksellers and printers in the 17th and 18th centuries. Supplementary paper. No. 3. *Western Antiquary*, 10 (1890–91), p. 11.
18. Plomer, *op. cit.*, p. 98. Wiles, *op. cit.*, pp. 16, 412–14.
19. David Stoker. The establishment of printing in Norwich. Causes and effects 1660–1760. *TCBS*, 7 (1977), pp. 94–111.
20. *Ibid.*, p. 97.
21. H. R. Plomer. James Abree, printer and bookseller, of Canterbury. *The Library*, 3rd ser., 4 (1913), pp. 46–56. Wiles, *op. cit.*, pp. 397–98. David Shaw. *Books printed or published by James Abree*. Canterbury, 1981. P.R.O. PROB 11/114/183.
22. Norman Taylor. Derbyshire printing and printers before 1800. *Journal of the Derbyshire Archaeological and Natural History Society*, 23 (1950), p. 39.
23. John Feather. Country book trade apprentices 1710–1760. *Publishing History*, 6 (1980), p. 98. S. F. Watson. Some materials for a history of printing and publishing in Ipswich. *Proceedings of the Suffolk Institute of Archaeology and Natural History*, 24 (1946–47), p. 199.
24. Wiles, *op. cit.*; and G. A. Cranfield. *The development of the provincial newspaper*. Oxford, 1962.
25. B.L. MS Add. 5853, ff. 106^{v}–107^{r}.
26. *The Northampton Mercury*, vol. 1, no. 5 (31 May 1720).
27. Wiles, *op. cit.*, pp. 96–100.
28. *Ibid.*, pp. 487–88.
29. *Ibid.*, pp. 127–28.
30. Freshwater, *op. cit.*, Pt 1, p. 16. Plomer, *op. cit.*, p. 296. Plomer, Bushnell, and Dix., *op. cit.*, p. 249.
31. Plomer, *op. cit.*, p. 318.

32. *Ibid.*, p. 259. Plomer, Bushnell, and Dix, *op. cit.*, p. 220. Wiles, *op. cit.*, p. 513.

33. *Ibid.*, pp. 472–73. The list of country agents can be checked against Plomer, *op. cit.*, and Plomer, Bushnell, and Dix, *op. cit.*

34. Wiles, *op. cit.*, pp. 452–53, compared with Hunt, *op. cit.*

35. Wiles, *op. cit.*, pp. 95–146.

36. *Ibid.*, 'Chronological Table', opposite p. 373.

37. See Chapter 4, pp. 44–68.

38. C. Lennart Carlson. *The first magazine. A history of The Gentleman's Magazine*. Providence, R. I., 1938, pp. 60–61.

39. R. M. Wiles. *Serial publication in England before 1750*. Cambridge, 1957, pp. 105–32.

40. D. C. Coleman. *The British paper industry 1495–1860*. Oxford, 1958, pp. 89–100.

41. *The Leeds Mercury*, vol. 2, no. 106 (10 Jan. 1769).

42. P.R.O. PROB 11/1115/171.

43. Hunt, *op. cit.*, pp. 49–50, 83–84. Richard Welford. Thomas Slack. *Archaeologia Aeliana*, 3rd ser., 17 (1920), pp. 145–51. Richard Welford. *Men of mark 'twixt Tyne and Tweed*. London, 3 vols., 1895, vol. 2, pp. 543–55.

44. Bodleian Library, Oxford. MS Top. Oxon. d. 247, f. 97. Wiles, *Freshest advices*, pp. 477–68. Harry Carter. *A history of the Oxford University Press*, vol. 1. *To the year 1780*. Oxford, 1975, p. 323, gives the date, wrongly, as 1741.

45. Carter, *op. cit.*, p. 361.

46. *Ibid.*, p. 324.

47. Nichols, *op. cit.*, vol. 3, pp. 398, 679.

48. P.R.O. PROB 11/1262/389.

49. There is a brief account of Goadby in *DNB*, but the best is by Nichols, *op. cit.*, vol. 3, pp. 435, 723–25.

50. Feather, Country book trade apprentices, p. 98, no. A19.

51. Wiles, *Freshest advices*, pp. 495–97, 510.

52. P.R.O. PROB 11/1045/357.

53. See below, Chapter 5, pp. 69–97.

54. Taylor, *op. cit.*, p. 54.

55. Wiles, *Freshest advices*, pp. 484–86.

56. Plomer, Bushnell, and Dix, *op. cit.*, p. 81.

57. Bodleian Library, Oxford. MS Eng. lett. c. 356, f. 26.

58. P.R.O. PROB 11/805/314.

59. C. H. Timperley. *Encyclopaedia of literary and typographical anecdote*. London, 1842, p. 785.

60. William B. Todd and Peter J. Wallis. Provincial booksellers c. 1744: the *Harleian Miscellany* subscription list. *The Library*, 5th ser., 29 (1974), p. 431.

61. Plomer, Bushnell, and Dix, *op. cit.*, p. 204.

62. *Ibid.*

63. See above, pp. 4–5.
64. D. F. McKenzie. *Stationers' Company apprentices 1700–1800*. Oxford (Oxford Bibliographical Society, new ser., 19), 1978, no. 6442.
65. P.R.O. PROB 11/1153/230.
66. For Pote's family, as a supplement to information in his will, see Austen-Leigh, *op. cit.*, pp. 132–33; and Nichols, *op. cit.*, vol. 3, pp. 418–19.
67. See above, p. 13 and note 6.
68. Plomer, Bushnell, and Dix, *op. cit.*, p. 129. Trade card in Bodleian Library, Oxford. John Johnson Collection. Sun, Alliance and London Insurance Group, London. Archives, 'Records of old agencies' file.
69. See below, pp. 83–87.
70. Plomer, Bushnell, and Dix, *op. cit.*, pp. 176–77.
71. For Mountfort and Feepound, see below, pp. 75–80.
72. Essex R.O. D/APb R 1/20. Plomer, Bushnell, and Dix, *op. cit.*, pp. 145–46.
73. Gloucestershire R.O. 1754/176. Plomer, Bushnell, and Dix, *op. cit.*, p. 248.
74. *John Cheney and his successors*. Banbury, 1936. Christopher R. Cheney. Early Banbury chapbooks and broadsides. *The Library*, 4th ser., 17 (1937), pp. 98–108. Some of the early records of the business are still extant in the firm's archives at Banbury, and my account of Cheney here and elsewhere is based on a re-examination of those records which were, of course, used also for the two works cited here.
75. Trevor Fawcett. Eighteenth-century Norfolk booksellers: a survey and register. *TCBS*, 6 (1972), p. 18.
76. J. C. Trewin and E. M. King. *Printer to the House*. London, 1952, p. 19.
77. Stanley Godman. A collection of Lewes handbills. *Sussex Archaeological Collections*, 97 (1959), pp. 58–68.
78. A. H. Arkle. Early Liverpool printers. *Transactions of the Historic Society of Lancashire and Cheshire*, 68 (1916), pp. 73–84. See, for example, Arkle's account of Adam and John Sadler (pp. 76–78) who printed from 1764 to 1789 but never had a newspaper.
79. *Records of the Borough of Nottingham*. Nottingham, 9 vols., 1882–1900, vol. 7, pp. 88, 150, 410–15.
80. Plomer, Bushnell, and Dix, *op. cit.*, p. 122.
81. John Daniel Leader (ed.). *The records of the Burgery of Sheffield*. London, 1897, p. 369. Plomer, Bushnell, and Dix, *op. cit.*, p. 101.
82. Samuel Johnson. *'The Idler' and 'The Rambler'*, ed. W. J. Bate, John M. Bullitt, and L. F. Powell. New Haven, Conn., 1963, p. 94.
83. 'Some thoughts on the Oxford Press', in I. G. Philip. *William Blackstone and the reform of the Oxford University Press in the eighteenth century*. Oxford (Oxford Bibliographical Society, new ser., 7), 1957, p. 23.
84. Joseph Hunter (ed.). *The life of Mr. Thomas Gent, printer of York; written by himself*. London, 1832, pp. 20–21.

85. Clough, *op. cit.* Freshwater, *op. cit.* Hunt, *op. cit.* Plomer, *op. cit.* David Stoker. A history of the Norwich book trades from 1660 to 1760. Library Association Fellowship thesis, 1976. Peter John Wallis. *An eighteenth-century book trade index.* Newcastle-upon-Tyne (PHIBB, 140), 1977. John Walton. A survey of the printing trade and related occupations in Nottingham and Nottinghamshire to 1900. Library Association Fellowship thesis, 1968. The problem is that Plomer, the only *national* survey, is hopelessly defective. Where we can compare his findings with those of more recent local investigators, we discover that he often records fewer than half of the number of persons in the trade. For example, for Norwich he records fifteen traders in the period 1700–25, while Stoker has twenty-seven; in Northumberland and Durham, 1700–25, Plomer has ten, Hunt twenty-two; in Nottinghamshire in the same period, Plomer has nine, Walton sixteen.
86. Wallis and Todd, *op. cit.*, pp. 421–40.
87. See below, p. 67.
88. See Jane E. Norton. *Guide to the national and provincial directories of England and Wales, excluding London, published before 1856.* London, 1950, pp. 32–34. Some cities, however, had local directories which were used as unverified, and sometimes outdated, sources: *ibid.*, nos. 491, 617, 711, 782, 816, 817, 850. See also Benjamin Walker. Birmingham directories. *Birmingham Archaeological Society Transactions*, 58 (1954), p. 21. At its worst, *UBD* omits eleven traders in Norwich out of a total of fifteen and six out of twenty-one in Newcastle-upon-Tyne. But it is generally far better than this; in all, about 10–15% of book traders in County Durham, Northumberland, Nottinghamshire, and the five west midland counties are omitted, and I have taken this as the national average.
89. W. G. Rimmer. The industrial profile of Leeds, 1740–1800. *Publications of the Thorseby Society*, 50 (1968), pp. 156–57.
90. Hunt, *op. cit.* Peter John Wallis. *The north-east book trade to 1860. Imprints and subscriptions.* Newcastle-upon-Tyne (PHIBB, 153), 1977; 2nd ed. (PHIBB, 268a), 1981.
91. *Sketchley's Bristol directory.* Bristol, 1775.
92. *Matthews new Bristol directory for the year 1793–4.* Bristol, 1794.
93. *The Liverpool directory for the year 1766.* Liverpool, 1766. *The Liverpool directory for the year 1774.* Liverpool, 1774. M. R. Perkin (ed.). *The book trade in Liverpool to 1805: a directory.* Liverpool (Book Trade in the North West Project), 1981.
94. W. G. Mitchinson. Bristol – metropolis of the west in the eighteenth century. *Transactions of the Royal Historical Society*, 5th ser., 11 (1954), pp. 88–89. T. C. Barker. Lancashire coal, Cheshire salt and the rise of Liverpool. *Transactions of the Historic Society of Lancashire and Cheshire*, 103 (1951), pp. 83–101.
95. The bankruptcy figures are from: P.R.O. B 4/1–20 (1710–71); *The London Gazette* (1772–85); William Smith & Co. *A list of bankrupts . . .*

from Jan. 1, 1766, to June 24, 1806. London, 1806 (1786–1800). For the complex subject of eighteenth-century bankruptcy laws, and especially the general desire to avoid the courts, see E. Welbourne. Bankruptcy before the era of Victorian reform. *Cambridge Historical Journal*, 4 (1932). A few specific cases are investigated below, pp. 93–96.

96. B. R. Mitchell and Phyllis Deane. *Abstract of British historical statistics*. Cambridge, 2nd ed., 1971, pp. 245–46.

97. Smith, *op. cit.*

98. A comparison of *UBD* and the 1801 census, a very crude exercise, suggests that a member of the book trade needed an immediate urban market of between 1,500 and 2,500 to have a viable business.

99. Nichols, *op. cit.*, vol. 3, p. 687n.

100. P.R.O. PROB 11/1529/557.

101. Bristol R.O. Will 1786 (Brown).

102. Guildhall Library, London, MS 11937/3, pp. 76–77; MS 11937/7, pp. 558–59.

103. P.R.O. PROB 11/1473/105.

CHAPTER 3. THE MARKET FOR BOOKS

1. Penelope Corfield. A provincial capital in the late seventeenth century: the case of Norwich. *In* Peter Clark and Paul Slack (ed.). *Crisis and order in English towns 1500–1700*. London, 1972, pp. 263–310.

2. C. W. Chalklin. *The provincial towns of Georgian England*. London, 1974, pp. 3–31.

3. It ought to be added that the whole question of literacy is still a matter of controversy among historians. For recent work, see David Cressy. *Literacy and the social order*. Cambridge, 1980.

4. Richard D. Altick. *The English common reader*. Chicago, 1957, pp. 30–41. R. K. Webb. *The British working class reader*. London, 1955, pp. 13–35.

5. D. F. McKenzie and J. C. Ross (ed.). *A ledger of Charles Ackers*. Oxford (Oxford Bibliographical Society, new ser., 15), 1968, pp. 249–52.

6. R. C. Alston. *A bibliography of the English language from the invention of printing to the year 1800*, vol. 4. *Spelling books*. Bradford, 1967, nos. 223–79.

7. Staffordshire R.O. Q/5B 1776, Debtors Trans. 1776. See below, pp. 79–80; and Appendix I.

8. Last leaf of Thomas Gent. *The ancient and modern history of the famous city of York*. York, 1730.

9. Advertisement in Patrick Sanderson. *The antiquities of the abbey or cathedral church of Durham*. Newcastle-upon-Tyne, 1767.

10. Issued from the address to which he moved on 12 June 1788; copy in the Cheney archives.

11. Northamptonshire R.O. D. 2727, f. 50^v.

12. H. McLachlan. *English education under the Test Acts*. Manchester, 1931.

13. Feather, John Clay, pp. 198–99, 202.
14. See below, pp. 115–17.
15. M. L. Clarke. *Classical education in Britain 1500–1900*. Cambridge, 1959, pp. 46–60.
16. Nicholas Hans. *New trends in education in the eighteenth century*. London, 1951, pp. 63–116.
17. Zena Crouch and Brian Simon. Private schools of Leicester and the county 1780–1840. *In* Brian Simon (ed.). *Education in Leicestershire 1540–1940*. Leicester, 1968, pp. 99, 111.
18. E. G. R. Taylor. *Mathematical practitioners of Hanoverian England 1714–1840*. Cambridge, 1966. P. J. Wallis. *An index of British mathematicians*, Part 2. *1701–60*. Newcastle-upon-Tyne (PHIBB, 105), 1976.
19. David M. Walker. *The Oxford companion to law*. Oxford, 1980, p. 659. *DNB* (Jacob).
20. Feather, John Clay, pp. 202–03.
21. See below, pp. 85–87.
22. John Cheney and Sons Ltd., Banbury. Archives. Account Book 1794–1800, pp. 24, 25, 27–28, 45–46, 63, 75–76.
23. Wiles, *Serial publication*, pp. 79–80, 270–71.
24. *Ibid.*, pp. 288, 289, 305, 322, 350.
25. Donald Read. *Press and people 1790–1850. Opinion in three English Cities*. London, 1961, deals with the crucial period in the development of an independent, and largely radical, provincial press.
26. Wiles, *Freshest advices*, pp. 149–86.
27. Some examples of local stories can be found in Clifford Morsley. *News from the English countryside 1750–1850*. London, 1979, pp. 13–148.
28. For distribution and its problems see: William F. Belcher. The sale and distribution of *The British Apollo*. *In* Richmond P. Bond (ed.). *Studies in the early English periodical*. Chapel Hill, N.C., 1957, pp. 73–101. Michael Harris. Newspaper distribution during Queen Anne's reign. Charles Delafaye and the Secretary of State's Office. *In* R. W. Hunt, I. G. Philip, and R. J. Roberts (ed.). *Studies in the book trade*. Oxford (Oxford Bibliographical Society, new ser., 18), 1975, pp. 139–51. J. M. Price. A note on the circulation of the London press 1700–1714. *BIHR*, 31 (1958), pp. 215–24. Henry L. Snyder. The circulation of newspapers in the reign of Queen Anne. *The Library*, 5th ser., 23 (1968), pp. 206–35. James R. Sutherland. The circulation of newspapers and literary periodicals. *The Library*, 4th ser., 15 (1934–35), pp. 110–24.
29. *Calendar of Treasury Papers 1720–1728*. London, 1889, p. 421.
30. *Parliamentary Papers* (1807), vol. 2, p. 219.
31. *Ibid.* (1806), vol. 7, pp. 811–14. Brian Austen. *English provincial posts, 1633–1840*. Chichester, 1978, pp. 99–100. See also below, pp. 47–48.
32. See below, pp. 117–18.
33. Wiles, *Serial publication*, pp. 286–94.
34. Belanger, *op. cit.*, pp. 285–95.

35. Richard Landon. Small profits do great things: James Lackington and eighteenth-century bookselling. *Studies in Eighteenth-Century Culture*, 5 (1976), pp. 378–99. The best account, however, is still Lackington's own in his *Memoirs of the first forty-five years of the life of James Lackington*. London, 1791.
36. *Ibid.*, pp. 91–93.
37. *Ibid.*, p. 40.
38. For a provincial edition of *Pilgrim's Progress*, see above, p. 6.
39. Feather, John Clay, p. 202.
40. *The works of Samuel Johnson*. 12 vols., London, rev. ed., 1816, vol. 7, p. 26. (*Idler*, no. 7, 27 May 1758).
41. A. S. Collins. *Authorship in the days of Johnson*. London, 1927, pp. 249–50.
42. Victor E. Neuburg. The Diceys and the chapbook trade. *The Library*, 5th ser., 24 (1969), pp. 219–31.
43. *Ibid.*, pp. 223–24. Frances M. Thompson. *Newcastle chapbooks*. Newcastle-upon-Tyne, 1969. Cheney, *op. cit.* Feather, John Clay, pp. 205–06. See below, pp. 106–08.
44. Arthur Roberts (ed.). *Letters of Hannah More to Zachary Macaulay*. London, 1860, pp. 427–28.
45. G. H. Spinney. Cheap Repository Tracts: Hazard and Marshall edition. *The Library*, 4th ser., 20 (1939–40), p. 296.
46. *The Monthly Magazine*, 11 (1801), p. 238.
47. Paul Kaufman. The community library: a chapter in English social history. *Transactions of the American Philosophical Society*, 57:2 (1967), pp. 12–13.
48. John Feather. The Ely Pamphlet Club 1766–1776. *TCBS*, 7 (1980), pp. 457–63. For a general account of the book clubs, see Paul Kaufman. English book clubs and their role in social history. *Libri*, 14 (1964–65), pp. 1–31.
49. Paul Kaufman. A bookseller's record of eighteenth-century book clubs. *The Library*, 5th ser., 15 (1960), pp. 278–87.
50. Hubert Collar. An eighteenth-century Essex book society. *Essex Review*, 44 (1935), pp. 109–12.
51. Frank Beckwith. The eighteenth-century proprietary library in England. *Journal of Documentation*, 3 (1947–48), pp. 81–98.
52. See, for example, *The Leeds Library 1768–1968*. Dewsbury, 1968, p. 116. P. Macintyre. Historical sketch of the Liverpool Library. *Transactions of the Historic Society of Lancashire and Cheshire*, 9 (1856–57), pp. 235–44. Charles Parrish. *History of the Birmingham Library*. London, 1966, p. 49.
53. Paul Kaufman. *Borrowings from the Bristol Library 1771–1784*. Charlottesville, Va., 1960, pp. 121–28.
54. Paul Kaufman. In defense of fair readers. *Review of English Literature*, 8:2 (1967), pp. 68–76. Kaufman, Community, p. 13.
55. Feather, Ely, pp. 460–62. Kathleen Hapgood. Library practice in the

Bristol Library Society 1772–1830. *Library History*, 5 (1981), pp. 147, 148.
56. See Alan Everitt. Kentish family portrait: an aspect of the rise of the pseudo-gentry. *In* Chalklin and Havinden, *op. cit.*, pp. 169–99.

CHAPTER 4. THE DISTRIBUTION SYSTEM

1. Graham Pollard and Albert Ehrman. *The distribution of books by catalogue*. Cambridge, 1965, pp. 163–77.
2. Theodore Besterman. *The beginnings of systematic bibliography*. Oxford, 1935, pp. 27–29, 38–39. Graham Pollard. Bibliographical aids to research. IV. General lists of books printed in England. *BIHR*, 12 (1934–35), pp. 164–74.
3. Hunt, *op. cit.*, p. 60. *DNB* (London).
4. D. F. Foxon. Monthly catalogues of books published. *The Library*, 5th ser., 18 (1963), pp. 223–28. Carlson, *op. cit.*, pp. 43–46.
5. *Ibid.*, pp. 53, 66–67.
6. *Ibid.*, pp. 8–10; and above, pp. 19–21.
7. Hodgson and Blagden, *op. cit.*, pp. 128, 134, 142, 150, 151, 152, 160, 191, 209 (Clavell); 121, 132, 142, 144, 158, 166, 174 (Lintot).
8. Sutherland, *op. cit.*, pp. 116–18.
9. Price, *op. cit.*, p. 220.
10. David Nichol Smith. The newspaper. *In* A. S. Turberville (ed.). *Johnson's England*. Oxford, 2 vols., 1933, vol. 2, pp. 359–60.
11. Yale University, Lewis Collection, Farmington, Conn. MS Minute Book of the proprietors of *The General Evening Post, passim*.
12. The nine newspapers selected for this survey are: *The London Courant* (*LC*); *The London Chronicle* (*LChron*); *The Morning Chronicle* (*MC*); *The St James's Chronicle* (*StJC*); *Berrow's Worcester Journal* (*BWJ*); *The Cambridge Chronicle and Journal* (*CCJ*); *The Leeds Mercury* (*LM*); *The Northampton Mercury* (*NM*); and *The York Courant* (*YC*).
13. *DNB* (Fawcett). John Fawcett, the younger. *An account of the life, ministry, and writings of the late rev. John Fawcett*. London, 1818.
14. John Paul. *The parish officer's complete guide*, new ed.: *YC*, 1833 (18 Jan. 1780), 1834 (25 Jan. 1780).
15. John Paul. *Every landlord or tenant his own lawyer*: *YC, ibid.* William Newnam. *The complete conveyancer, part 1*: *BWJ*, 4465 (13 Jan. 1780), 4467 (17 Jan. 1780); *CCJ*, 897 (1 Jan. 1780), 898 (8 Jan. 1780), 900 (22 Jan. 1780), *NM*, 60:44 (10 Jan. 1780), 60:47 (31 Jan. 1780); *YC*, 1834 (25 Jan. 1780).
16. John Paul. *A digest of laws relating to ... game*, new ed.: *YC*, 1833 (18 Jan. 1780), 1834 (25 Jan. 1780).
17. Thomas Bateman, *An appendix to the treatise on agistment tithe*: *CCJ*, 899 (15 Jan. 1780), 900 (22 Jan. 1780); and *NM*, 60:46 (24 Jan. 1780), 60:47 (31 Jan. 1780).
18. Walter Robinson, *Every master and servant his own lawyer*, and the same

author's *The landlord's pocket lawyer*: *LChron*, 3603 (4 Jan. 1780), 3605 (8 Jan. 1780), 3607 (13 Jan. 1780); *StJC*, 2944 (22 Jan. 1780); *BWJ*, 4464 (6 Jan. 1780), 4465 (13 Jan. 1780); *CCJ*, 898 (8 Jan. 1780), 899 (15 Jan. 1780); *NM*, 60:44 (10 Jan. 1780), 60:45 (17 Jan. 1780); and *YC*, 1833 (18 Jan. 1780), 1834 (25 Jan. 1780); and William Sheppard, *The touchstone of common assurances*, 4th ed.: *LChron*, 3611 (25 Jan. 1780), 3612 (27 Jan. 1780); *BWJ*, 4467 (27 Jan. 1780); *CCJ*, 900 (22 Jan. 1780), and *YC*, 1834 (25 Jan. 1780).

19. *BWJ*, 4466 (20 Jan. 1780); *CCJ*, 899 (15 Jan. 1780), 900 (22 Jan. 1780); *LM*, 678 (18 Jan. 1780); *NM*, 60:45 (17 Jan. 1780), 60:46 (24 Jan. 1780); *LChron*, 3609 (18 Jan. 1780), 3611 (25 Jan. 1780); *MC*, 3330 (20 Jan. 1780), 3337 (28 Jan. 1780); and *StJC*, 2946 (27 Jan. 1780). The prospectuses are Bodleian Library, Oxford. J. Pros. 262, 263, 267, 275 and 288.

20. *BWJ*, 4466 (20 Jan. 1780), 4467 (27 Jan. 1780); *CCJ*, 900 (22 Jan. 1780); *NM*, 60:46 (24 Jan. 1780), 60:47 (31 Jan. 1780); *YC*, 1833 (18 Jan. 1780); *LC* (20 Jan. 1780), (27 Jan. 1780), (29 Jan. 1780); *LChron*, 3610 (*bis*) (22 Jan. 1780), 3611 (25 Jan. 1780), 3612 (27 Jan. 1780); *MC*, 3330 (20 Jan. 1780), 3332 (22 Jan. 1780), 3334 (25 Jan. 1780), 3336 (27 Jan. 1780), 3338 (29 Jan. 1780); *StJC*, 2942 (18 Jan. 1780), 2945 (25 Jan. 1780), 2947 (29 Jan. 1780).

21. *The Political Magazine*: *CCJ*, 898 (8 Jan. 1780), 899 (15 Jan. 1780), 901 (29 Jan. 1780); *NM*, 60:47 (31 Jan. 1780); *Shakespeare*: *CCJ*, 897 (1 Jan. 1780); *LC* (3 Jan. 1780); *MC* 3326 (3) (15 Jan. 1780); *The Novelist's Magazine*: *MC* 3338 (31 Jan. 1780).

22. *NM*, 60:47 (31 Jan. 1780); *YC*, 1834 (25 Jan. 1780); *LC* (25 Jan. 1780), (29 Jan. 1780); *LChron*, 3609 (18 Jan. 1780), 3610 (20 Jan. 1780), 3612 (27 Jan. 1780); *MC*, 3336 (27 Jan. 1780), 3338 (29 Jan. 1780), 3340 (31 Jan. 1780).

23. Walter Graham. *English literary periodicals*. New York, 1930, pp. 208–15.

24. Lewis M. Knapp. *Tobias Smollett, doctor of men and manners*. Princeton, N.J., 1949, pp. 170–81. Lewis M. Knapp (ed.). *The letters of Tobias Smollett*. Oxford, 1970, pp. 68–70.

25. Feather, Ely, p. 459.

26. A. N. L. Munby and Lenore Coral. *British book sale catalogues 1676–1800*. London, 1977, p. 42.

27. Nichols, *op. cit.*, vol. 3, 626. Pollard and Ehrman, *op. cit.*, pp. 156–57.

28. *Ibid.*, pp. 178–95. Sarah L. C. Clapp. The beginning of subscription publication in the seventeenth century. *MP*, 29 (1931–32), pp. 199–224. John Feather. *Book prospectuses before 1801 in the John Johnson collection*. Oxford, 1976, pp. 1–5. The whole subject is dealt with at greater length in John Feather. *The English book prospectus: an illustrated history*. Minneapolis, 1984.

29. Franklin B. Williams. Scholarly publication in Shakespeare's day: a leading case. *In* James G. McManaway, Giles E. Dawson, and Edwin E.

Willoughby. *John Quincy Adams memorial studies*. Washington, D.C., 1948, p. 767.

30. Bodleian Library, Oxford. J. Pros. 204.
31. *DNB* (King). Nichols, *op. cit.*, vol. 9, p. 169.
32. There are two prospectuses, to be dated 1774 and late 1776, in B.L. 1879. b. 1 (vol. 1).
33. Northamptonshire R.O. D. 2928, 21 Feb. 1781.
34. J. A. Venn and J. Venn. *Alumni Cantabrigienses*, Part 1. *From the earliest times to 1751*. Cambridge, 4 vols., 1922–27, vol. 2, p. 379.
35. The clergyman, under the pseudonym 'Clericus', contributed a note on Hitchcock to John Nichols's *History of Leicestershire* (vol. 4, p. 47, n. 5). See also *VCH Leics.*, vol. 1, p. 392; *The Gentleman's Magazine*, 59 (1789), pp. 180–81.
36. *DNB* (Harrod); see also below, pp. 111–13.
37. Bodleian Library, Oxford. MS Engl lett. c. 357, f. 188.
38. Bodleian Library, Oxford. MS Eng. lett. c. 355, f. 71.
39. Bodleian Library, Oxford. MS Eng. lett. b. 18, f. 69.
40. Bodleian Library, Oxford. MS Eng. lett. c. 355, f. 71.
41. Lackington, *op. cit.*, p. 214.
42. On this complex subject, see L. S. Pressnell. *Country banking in the industrial revolution*. Oxford, 1956.
43. Humberside R.O. SCR 441, p. 109.
44. Bodleian Library, Oxford. MS Eng. lett. c. 21, f. 95^v.
45. *Ibid.*, f. 85.
46. P.R.O. C 104/47, vol. M, ff. 111^v–15^r.
47. Bodleian Library, Oxford. MS Eng. lett. c. 356, f. 26.
48. Bodleian Library, Oxford. MS Eng. lett. c. 357, f. 183.
49. Bodleian Library, Oxford. MS Gough Gen. Top. 47, f. 238.
50. R. W. Chapman (ed.). *The letters of Samuel Johnson*. Oxford, 3 vols., 1952, vol. 2, pp. 112–15. R. W. Chapman. Authors and booksellers. *In* Turberville, *op. cit.*, vol. 2, p. 315.
51. Barnes, *op. cit.*, p. 52.
52. Cambridge University Library. Munby Collection, MS Book Trade Letters 1, no. E2.
53. *Monthly Review*, 2nd ser., 22 (1797), p. 121.
54. Belanger, *op. cit.*, *passim*.
55. D. F. Foxon discussed this in the first of his Lyell Lectures on *Pope and the eighteenth-century book trade*, delivered at Oxford in 1976. Unfortunately, this masterly work is not yet published, but a typescript is available at the Bodleian Library. It was not, however, to Foxon's purpose to discuss marketing generally, as I have tried to do here. See also Michael Treadwell. London trade publishers 1675–1750. *The Library*, 6th ser., 4 (1982), pp. 99–134.
56. I shall avoid the use of the word 'publisher' in this section. In this example, Y is what we should now call the 'publisher': the financier and organiser with the legal right to issue the book. But in the eighteenth

century, Z would have been called the 'publisher', since it was he who distributed, or 'published', the book, in the sense in which, in legal terminology, a libel can be 'published' by the distributor or seller as well as the author, the printer, or the financier/organiser.

57. Philip Macquer. *A chronological abridgment of the Roman history*, translated by John Nugent.

58. Maxted, *op. cit.*, pp. 37, 216–17.

59. George F. Black. Macpherson's Ossian and the Ossianic controversy. *BNYPL*, 30 (1926), p. 425.

60. John Owen. *An exposition of the Epistle to the Hebrews.*

61. Emanuel Swedenborg. *Concerning the earths in our solar system.*

62. Thomas Vivian. *An exposition of the catechism of the Church of England.*

63. Joseph Forster. *Alumni Oxonienses: the members of the University of Oxford, 1715–1886.* Oxford, 4 vols., 1887, vol. 4, p. 1475. George Clement Boase and William Prideaux Courtney. *Bibliotheca Cornubiensis.* London, 3 vols., 1874–82, vol. 2, pp. 836–37.

64. William Shaw. *A Galic and English dictionary.*

65. W. T. Jackman. *The development of transportation in modern England.* Cambridge, 2 vols., 1916, vol. 1, pp. 304–05. Edwin A. Pratt. *A history of inland transport and communication.* London, 1912, p. 36. William Albert. *The turnpike road system in England 1663–1840.* Cambridge, 1972, pp. 30–56.

66. Matthews, *op. cit.*, pp. 94–98.

67. John Copeland. *Roads and their traffic 1750–1850.* Newton Abbot, 1968, p. 81.

68. Jackman, *op. cit.*, vol. 1, p. 140, n. 1.

69. Bodleian Library, Oxford. MS Eng. lett. b. 18, f. 69.

70. Cambridge University Library. Munby Collection, MS Book Trade Letters 1, no. P6.

71. Bodleian Library, Oxford. MS Eng. lett. c. 357, f. 188.

72. Theodore Besterman. *The publishing firm of Cadell and Davies.* Oxford, 1938, p. 113.

73. P.R.O. PROB 11/1326/483. Cruttwell had four shares in the Kennet and Avon Canal, which linked the Thames at Reading to the Avon at Bristol, via Bath. See Kenneth R. Clew. *The Kennet and Avon Canal.* Newton Abbot, 1968, pp. 73, 84.

74. William Dunn Macray. *Annals of the Bodleian Library.* Oxford, 2nd ed., 1890, p. 211.

75. The catalogue was that which included books from Sterne's library; Munby and Coral, *op. cit.*, p. 66. Bodleian Library, Oxford. MS Eng. lett. c. 20, f. 110.

76. Bodleian Library, Oxford. MS Eng. lett. c. 20, f. 28; MS Eng. lett. c. 21, f. 85.

77. Feather, John Clay, pp. 207–08.

78. *The Northampton Mercury*, 41:48 (23 Feb. 1761).

79. *Berrow's Worcester Journal*, 2655 (26 June 1760).

80. Francis Fawkes (ed.). *The holy Bible*. London, 1761–62.
81. John Pendred. *The earliest directory of the book trade*. Ed. Graham Pollard. London (Supplement to the Bibliographical Society's Transactions, 14), 1955, pp. xi–xvi.
82. *Ibid.*, pp. xviii–xix.
83. *Ibid.*, pp. 43–48.
84. *Ibid.*, pp. 22–37.
85. These three are in Birmingham (Swinney: *Birmingham and Stafford Chronicle*); Chester (Fletcher: *Chester Chronicle*); and York (Blanchard: *York Chronicle*). The other two are Green and Gedge (Bury St Edmunds: *Bury St Edmunds and Bury Post*); and Bladgen (Winchester: *Salisbury and Winchester Journal*). Both had London agents, and may be accidental omissions by Pendred.

CHAPTER 5. THE BOOKSELLING BUSINESS

1. R. Campbell. *The London tradesman*. London, 1747, p. 134.
2. Lackington, *op. cit.*, p. 278.
3. Nichols, *op. cit.*, p. 680n.
4. Reproduced in Sigfred Taubert. *Bibliopola. Bilder und Texte aus der Welt des Buchhandels*. Hamburg, 2 vols., 1966, vol. 2, p. 207.
5. *Ibid.*, vol. 2, p. 245.
6. Guildhall Library, London. MS 11937/7, p. 58.
7. Guildhall Library, London. MS 11937/9, f. 169^v.
8. Guildhall Library, London. MS 11937/10, p. 329.
9. *Ibid.*, p. 263.
10. Guildhall Library, London. MS 11937/3, pp. 76–77; MS 11937/7, pp. 557–59.
11. I. Steel. *The Hastings guide*. Hastings, 2nd ed., 1797, p. 38.
12. Staffordshire R.O. Q/5B 1776, Debtors Trans. 1776. See also note 38 below, and Appendix I.
13. Guildhall Library, London. MS 11937. Until 1793 the Registers of Policies do not distinguish between London and country customers, and until the index, at present in process of compilation, is available, to search them for a limited purpose such as the present one would be impractical. But the Country Registers from 1793 onwards do give a good idea of valuations at the end of the century when the trade was reaching its maximum point of expansion in the period covered by this book.
14. Guildhall Library, London. MS 11937/1, p. 87.
15. Guildhall Library, London. MS 11937/7, pp. 557–59.
16. In fact, forty-five out of ninety-one.
17. Twelve of the ninety-one.
18. Campbell, *op. cit.*, pp. 331–40. He suggested £500 to £5,000 as the range; for most trades he suggested about £100, and very rarely more than £1,000.

19. Alexander, *op. cit.*, pp. 206–07.
20. Boswell, *ed. cit.*, vol. 1, p. 57.
21. *Ibid.*, vol. 1, p. 36, n. 2.
22. 'I think that I have nothing new that will at present divert you.' The letter is printed in J. W. Whiston. Some letters and accounts of Michael Johnson. *Johnson Society Transactions* (1974), pp. 40–41.
23. H. R. Plomer. A Chester bookseller 1667–1700: some of his customers and the books he sold them. *The Library*, new ser., 4 (1903), pp. 373–83.
24. Bodleian Library, Oxford. John Johnson collection, trade card.
25. Munby and Coral, *op. cit.*, p. 29. The *Catalogue of choice books* is Bodleian Library, Oxford. 2591 f. 1. See also Nichols, *op. cit.*, vol. 3, p. 672.
26. Trewin and King, *op. cit.*, pp. 29–30.
27. Munby and Coral, *op. cit.*, p. 71.
28. William Hutton. *The life of William Hutton.* London, 1816, p. 77.
29. *Ibid.*, p. 75.
30. *Berrow's Worcester Journal*, 2636 (14 Feb. 1760).
31. Plomer, Bushnell, and Dix, *op. cit.*, pp. 176–77. Wallis, *Eighteenth-century*, p. 28. Freshwater, *op. cit.*, Pt 1, p. 12.
32. *VCH Worcs*, vol. 4, pp. 382, 457.
33. Sir Jeffrey Gilbert. *A treatise on rents.* London, 1758; and Sir William Blackstone. *Considerations on the question whether tenants by copy of Court Roll are freeholders.* London, 1758.
34. *The new compleat parish officer*, possibly an edition of the work by Giles Jacob, or of that by John Paul.
35. R. Boote. *Solicitor's guide and tradesman's instructor.* There were several editions.
36. *DNB* (Hurd).
37. William Henry McMenemey. *A history of the Worcester Royal Infirmary.* London, 1947, pp. 10–70.
38. The inventory (note 12, above) cannot be satisfactorily reproduced. Appendix I is a transcript of the list of books.
39. The catalogue in which some of these books had appeared seems not to be extant.
40. Nichols, *op. cit.*, vol. 3, p. 698 and n.
41. *Ibid.*, vol. 3, p. 673n.
42. *Ibid.*, vol. 3, p. 687n. Munby and Coral, *op. cit.*, index the catalogues on p. 144. Plomer, Bushnell, and Dix, *op. cit.*, p. 245.
43. Nichols, *op. cit.*, p. 678n.
44. *Ibid.*, vol. 3, pp. 675–77, and 675n.
45. Arkle, *op. cit.*, pp. 78–79; Perkin, *op. cit.*, p. 33.
46. Watson, *op. cit.*, p. 201.
47. Nichols, *op. cit.*, vol. 3, p. 674n; and p. 13, above, for Dagnall. See p. 22, above, for Jackson.
48. Bodleian Library, Oxford. John Johnson Collection, trade card.
49. Feather, John Clay, *passim.*

50. Coleman, *op. cit.*, pp. 88–100.
51. A. H. Shorter. *Papermaking in the British Isles*. Newton Abbot, 1971, pp. 31–34.
52. *Ibid.*, pp. 55–58.
53. Hutton, *op. cit.*, pp. 99, 110, 112.
54. *Ibid.*, pp. 216–19.
55. Richard W. Goulding. *Notes on Louth printers and booksellers of the eighteenth century*. Louth, 1917, p. 2. He also had a shop in Doncaster.
56. Bodleian Library, Oxford. John Johnson Collection, trade card.
57. *Ibid.* (Thorner). For Harrop, see p. 85, below.
58. Feather, John Clay, p. 201.
59. John Alden. Pills and publishing: some notes on the English book trade. *The Library*, 5th ser., 7 (1952), pp. 21–37.
60. Leslie H. Matthews. *History of pharmacy in Britain*. Edinburgh, 1962, pp. 285–88.
61. *Parliamentary Papers* (1845), vol. 48, p. 122. Welsh, *op. cit.*, pp. 21–23.
62. Arthur Sherbo. *Christopher Smart, scholar of the university*. East Lansing, Mich., 1967, p. 108.
63. Nichols, *op. cit.*, vol. 3, p. 387. Maxted, *op. cit.*, p. 17. The original patent, for Balsam of Life, is enrolled in *Parliamentary Papers* (1845), vol. 48, p. 121.
64. P. G. M. Dickson. *The Sun Insurance Office 1710–1960*. Oxford, 1960, pp. 68–70.
65. Sun, Alliance, and London Insurance Group, London. Archives, 'Records of old agencies' file.
66. Plomer, Bushnell, and Dix, *op. cit.*, p. 39.
67. Guildhall Library, London. MS 14386, f. 16^r.
68. Pendred, *ed. cit.*, p. 44.
69. Guildhall Library, London. MS 14386, f. 22^r.
70. Pendred, *ed. cit.*, p. 45.
71. *The Leeds Mercury*, 33:1718 (4 Jan. 1800). W. E. A. Axon (ed.). *The annals of Manchester*. Manchester, 1886, pp. 88–89. W. H. Challoner. Manchester in the latter half of the eighteenth century. *BJRL*, 46 (1959–60), pp. 57–58.
72. Dorothy Davis. *A history of shopping*. London, 1966, p. 228.
73. Janet Blackman. The development of the retail grocery trade in the nineteenth century. *Business History*, 9 (1967), pp. 110–17. J. Aubrey Rees. *The grocery trade: its history and romance*. London, 2 vols., 1910, vol. 2, p. 141.
74. S. Atkinson. *Chitty's Stamp Laws*. London, 3rd ed., 1850, pp. 1–4. Edward Hughes. The English stamp duties, 1664–1774. *EHR*, 56 (1941), pp. 234–64.
75. The whole splendid diatribe was published in *The Edinburgh Review*, 33 (1820), pp. 77–78.
76. Hume's speech in the House of Commons, 22 March 1821, in *Hansard*,

new ser., 4 (1821), col. 1401–11. For distribution and profits, see Hughes, *op. cit.*

77. Mary Moorman. *William Wordsworth, a biography. The later years 1805–1850.* Oxford, 1965, pp. 244–46.

78. See above, p. 18, note 35.

79. I am indebted to Mr D. F. Foxon, who has shared with me his great knowledge of the stamp duties.

80. These examples are taken from *The Universal British Directory.*

81. Hunt, *op. cit.*, p. 22.

82. Plomer, Bushnell, and Dix, *op. cit.*, p. 146.

83. Oxford University Archives. Chancellor's Court Wills, Vol. W–Y, Hyp./B/35.

84. *Ibid.*

85. McKerrow, *op. cit.*, pp. 170–71.

86. A. L. Reade. Samuel Richardson and his family circle. II. *NQ*, 12th ser., 11 (1922), pp. 224–26. T. C. Duncan Eaves and Ben D. Kimpel. *Samuel Richardson. A biography.* Oxford, 1971, p. 49.

87. P.R.O. PROB 11/908/148.

88. Richard Welford. Early Newcastle typography, 1639–1800. *Archaeologia Aeliana*, 3rd ser., 3 (1907), p. 52.

89. *The London Gazette*, 11890 (7–11 July 1778).

90. Fawcett, *op. cit.*, pp. 14, 17. Basil Cozens-Hardy and Ernest A. Kent. *The mayors of Norwich 1403 to 1835.* Norwich, 1938, p. 159. P.R.O. PROB 11/1292/406.

91. Margery M. Rowe and Andrew M. Jackson. *Exeter Freemen 1266–1967.* Exeter (Devon and Cornwall Record Society, extra ser., 1) 1967, pp. 203, 217, 223, 225, 226, 232, 234, 237, 239, 240, 241, 248, 262, 265, 268, 285, 286, 294, 300, 303, 304, 305, 306, 311, 312, 313, 314, 317, 321, 325, 328, 329, 332.

92. Francis Collins (ed.). *Register of the Freemen of the City of York*, Vol. 2. *1559–1759.* Durham (The Surtees Society, 102), 1900, pp. 184, 185, 191, 195, 214, 216, 217, 223, 233, 235, 236, 240, 242, 243, 252, 254, 256, 257, 260, 262, 263, 266, 271, 275, 278, 279, 280, 282, 285, 288. I am greatly indebted to Mr Alan Crossley of the Victoria County History for his advice on this and other aspects of urban history.

93. P.R.O. IR 1/41–53. Feather, Country book trade apprentices, *passim.*

94. Hunt, *op. cit.*, p. 95.

95. See above, p. 18.

96. Clements's will is Oxford University Archives. Chancellor's Court Wills, Vol. C, Hyp./B/23.

97. P.R.O. C 107/164.

98. *Records of the Borough of Nottingham*, vol. 7, p. 32.

99. *A catalogue of several libraries . . . to be sold at Tunbridge-Wells . . . 1754 . . . by Edmund Baker.* Tunbridge-Wells, 1754. This was a fixed-price, not an auction, catalogue, despite the form of words in the title.

100. *A catalogue of a valuable collection of books . . . on sale . . . 1790. By S.*

Tupman. Nottingham 1790. *A catalogue of books . . . 1789, at the shop of Ann Ireland.* Leicester, 1789. The latter, however, was considered underpriced; see p. 54, above.

101. *A catalogue of books . . . to be sold . . . 1789 . . . by John Binns.* Leeds, 1789.
102. Guildhall Library, London. MS 11937/2, p. 299.
103. *Ibid.*, p. 264.
104. Oxford University Archives. Chancellor's Court Inventories, Vol. R–S, Hyp./B/18. The relevant portion is transcribed in Appendix II.
105. For Seale, see John P. Chalmers. Bodleian copyright deposit survivors of the first sixteen years of the Copyright Act of Queen Anne 10 April 1710–25 March 1726. Oxford University D.Phil. thesis, 1974, pp. 42–44, 495–96.
106. P.R.O. PROB 11/1292/406.
107. P.R.O. PROB 11/1227/19.
108. P.R.O. PROB 11/805/314.
109. P.R.O. PROB 11/1473/105.
110. P.R.O. PROB 11/1545/310.
111. Oxford University Archives. Chancellor's Court Wills, Vol. Q–SH Hyp./B/32.
112. *Ibid.*, Vol. W–Y, Hyp./B/35.
113. P.R.O. PROB 11/1293/460.
114. Guildhall Library, London. MS 11937/7, p. 15.
115. Guildhall Library, London. MS 11937/5, p. 342.
116. Guildhall Library, London. MS 11937/9, p. 579.
117. P.R.O. PROB 11/915/217.
118. P.R.O. PROB 11/1302/11.
119. Guildhall Library, London. MS 11937/8, p. 267.
120. Guildhall Library, London. MS 11937/4, p. 145.
121. P.R.O. PROB 11/1504/755.
122. Guildhall Library, London. MS 11937/17.
123. P.R.O. PROB 11/1305/753; and Guildhall Library, London. MS 11937/10, p. 263.
124. Guildhall Library, London. MS 11937/4, p. 622.
125. Guildhall Library, London. MS 11937/14, p. 564.
126. P.R.O. PROB 11/1115/171.
127. Guildhall Library, London. MS 11937/12, p. 516.
128. Guildhall Library, London. MS 11937/7, p. 53.
129. Guildhall Library, London. MS 11937/8, p. 333.
130. P.R.O. PROB 11/1355/198. Roland Austin. Samuel Rudder. *The Library*, 3rd ser., 6 (1915), pp. 235–51.
131. *Records of the Borough of Nottingham*, vol. 7, pp. 298, 350, 410, 411, 415.
132. H. E. Forrest (ed.). *Shrewsbury Burgess Roll*. Shrewsbury, 1924, p. 25.
133. Collins, *op. cit.*, p. 191.

134. Nichols, *op. cit.*, vol. 3, pp. 443–44.
135. Timperley, *op. cit.*, p. 827.
136. A. Temple Patterson. *A history of Southampton 1700–1914. Vol. 1. An oligarchy in decline 1700–1835*. Southampton (Southampton Record Series, 11), 1966, pp. 78–89.
137. P.R.O. PROB 11/802/172.
138. Oxford University Archives. Chancellor's Court Wills, Vol. W–Y, Hyp./B/35.
139. Hutton, *op. cit.*, pp. 216, 219. R. B. Rose. The Priestley riots of 1791. *Past and Present*, 18 (1960), p. 74.
140. Kaufman, Community library, p. 14.
141. P.R.O. PROB 11/1457/197. J. E. Hutton. *A short history of the Moravian church*. London, 1895, *passim*. John Holmes. *History of the Protestant Church of the United Brethren*. London, 2 vols., 1825–30, vol. 2, p. 340.
142. B. L. MS Add. 15932, ff. 17–18, 24–27, 30–31.
143. Guildhall Library, London. MS 11937/19, p. 11. Hunt, *op. cit.*, p. 22.
144. Plomer, Bushnell, and Dix, *op. cit.*, p. 257. Joseph Hill. *The book makers of old Birmingham*. Birmingham, 1907, pp. 39–41.
145. Wiles, *Freshest advices*, p. 381.
146. Boswell, *ed. cit.*, vol. 1, pp. 85–87.
147. Chapman, *ed. cit.*, vol. 1, pp. 17–19, 70.
148. Birmingham Public Library. MS 19012, f. 5.
149. Carlson, *op. cit.*, pp. 25–26.
150. Gilbert J. French. *The life and times of Samuel Crompton*. Manchester, 2nd ed., 1880, pp. 246–60.
151. P.R.O. B 4/10/224.
152. French, *op. cit.*, pp. 293–94.
153. Hill, *op. cit.*, p. 45.
154. Plomer, Bushnell, and Dix, *op. cit.*, pp. 48–49, 255. Wiles, *Freshest advices*, p. 513. Gent, *op. cit.*, pp. 191–92. Davies, *op. cit.*, pp. 260–61, 291n, 311. P.R.O. B 4/11/91.
155. *The London Gazette*, 11736 (14–18 Jan. 1777). Davies, *op. cit.*, pp. 331–35.
156. *The London Gazette*, 11920 (12–14 Oct. 1778). Charles Herbert Mayo. *Bibliotheca Dorsetensis*. London, 1885, pp. 77–79.
157. P.R.O. PROB 11/1422/162. Guildhall Library, London. MS 11937/10, p. 323.
158. *The London Gazette*, 11851 (21–24 Feb. 1778). Patterson, *op. cit.*, pp. 41–42, 114–15.
159. *Pace* Joan Knott. Circulating libraries in Newcastle in the 18th and 19th centuries. *Library History*, 2 (1970–72), p. 234.
160. *The London Gazette*, 11325 (6–9 Feb. 1773).
161. James Clephan. More about early booksellers on the Tyne. *Monthly Chronicle of North Country Lore and Legend*, 1 (1887), pp. 412–15. Hunt, *op. cit.*, pp. 17, 21–22.

CHAPTER 6. THE PRINTING OFFICE

1. Gent, *op. cit.*, pp. 181–82.
2. J. J. Bagley (ed.). *The Great Diurnall of Nicholas Blundell*, Vol. 2. *1712–1719*. Liverpool (Record Society of Lancashire and Cheshire, 112), 1970, p. 25.
3. Arkle, *op. cit.*, pp. 75–76. Wiles, *Freshest advices*, pp. 434–35.
4. Pendred, *op. cit.*, p. 55.
5. Maxted, *op. cit.*, p. 5. W. B. Todd. *A directory of printers and others in allied trades. London and vicinity 1800–1840*. London, 1972, p. 5.
6. John Cheney and Sons, Ltd., Banbury. Archives. Notebook of Thomas Cheney, 1805.
7. Maxted, *op. cit.*, p. 48.
8. E. C. Bigmore and C. W. H. Wyman. *A bibliography of printing*. London, 3 vols., 1884–86, vol. 1, p. 232. Elizabeth Harris and Clinton Sisson. *The common press*. London, 1978, pp. 8–9.
9. Maxted, *op. cit.*, p. 85. Todd, *op. cit.*, p. 74.
10. Maxted, *op. cit.*, p. 128. Todd, *op. cit.*, p. 111.
11. Moxon, *ed. cit.*, p. 45.
12. James Watson. *History of the art of printing*. Edinburgh, 1713, pp. 7, 22.
13. A few years ago Dr Philip Gaskell did exactly this; his press is now in the Morison Room at Cambridge University Library.
14. James Moran. *Printing presses*. Berkeley and Los Angeles, 1978, pp. 40, 229. B. Woodcroft (ed.). *Patents for inventions. Abridgements of specifications relating to printing*. London, 1859, p. 88.
15. Cranfield, *op. cit.*, pp. 242–43. Davies, *op. cit.*, pp. 376–80.
16. Paul Morgan. *Warwickshire printers' notices 1799–1866*. Stratford-upon-Avon (Dugdale Society, 28), 1970, pp. 1–3.
17. P.R.O. PROB 11/1402/988.
18. See Appendix III.
19. McKenzie, *op. cit.*, vol. 1, p. 44; vol. 2, pp. 48, 237.
20. Carter, *op. cit.*, p. 386.
21. P.R.O. c 104/68/40.
22. Silvestre Bouchard. *Le manuel de l'imprimeur*. Paris, 1791, p. 93. The English price was calculated by Philip Gaskell. The decline of the common press. Cambridge University Ph.D. thesis, 1956, p. 179.
23. Caleb Stower. *The printer's grammar*. London, 1808, p. 516.
24. Moxon, *op. cit.*, pp. 25–26.
25. This is based on the late seventeenth-century price list in Bodleian Library, Oxford. MS. Rawl. D. 317^B, f. 163 (£309.3s.4d.); and prices paid by Cambridge University Press in 1699–1708, in McKenzie, *op. cit.*, vol. 1, p. 53 (£295.0s.0d.).
26. At the prices quoted by Stower, *op. cit.*, p. 514, the cost would have been £601.1s.5d.
27. F. C. Morgan. William Henry Parker's type specimens. *Transactions of the Woolhope Naturalists' Field Club*, 40 (1972), p. 390, Plates XII, XIII.

28. Pendred, *op. cit.*, pp. 5–6.
29. F. E. Pardoe. *John Baskerville of Birmingham.* London, 1975, pp. 23–27. Perhaps a note is needed on Baskerville. Clearly he was, in a strictly geographical sense, a provincial printer. But it is more useful to regard him as a gifted and wealthy amateur rather than the sort of printer under discussion here; in this he was unique. Consequently, I have not attempted any discussion of him, although he would, no doubt, have a significant place in a more general history of eighteenth-century English printing.
30. Edward Rowe Mores. *A dissertation upon English typographical founders and founderies, 1778.* Ed. Harry Carter and Christopher Ricks. Oxford, 1963, p. 80.
31. W. Turner Berry and A. F. Johnson. *Catalogue of specimens of printing types by English and Scottish printers and founders 1665–1830.* London, 1935, p. 32.
32. *Ibid.*, p. 71. W. Turner Berry and A. F. Johnson. A note on the literature of British type specimens, with a supplement to the Catalogue. *Signature*, new ser., 16 (1952), p. 37.
33. Berry and Johnson, *Catalogue*, p. 38.
34. Caslon; Caslon and Catherwood; Fry; Figgins; and Thorne. For this list, see note 6, above.
35. Trewin and King, *op. cit.*, pp. 27–28.
36. P.R.O. PROB 11/1045/357. D. F. McKenzie. *Stationers' Company apprentices 1701–1800.* Oxford (Oxford Bibliographical Society, new ser., 19), 1978, p. 142. Isaac Watts (McKenzie 3291) may also still have been with Goadby. One of the other journeymen, Benjamin Dodge, was another former apprentice (McKenzie 3286). The third was John Bettinson, who had been a partner in the old *Sherborne Mercury*. For Goadby see above, p. 22.
37. *Cambridge Chronicle and Journal*, 899 (15 Jan. 1780).
38. Bodleian Library, Oxford. MS Gough Gen. Top. 47, f. 206. Pardon was apprenticed to William Tooke of Clerkenwell (McKenzie, *Apprentices*, 8262).
39. John Child. *Industrial relations in the British printing industry.* London, 1967, pp. 98–104. Ellic Howe. *The London compositor.* London, 1947, p. 226. For tramping, see J. W. Rounsfell. *On the road. Journeys of a tramping printer.* Horsham, 1982.
40. Nichols, *op. cit.*, vol. 3, pp. 466–67.
41. Wiles, *Freshest advices*, p. 72.
42. *Ibid.*, pp. 105–06.
43. M. Dorothy George. *London life in the XVIIIth century.* London, 3rd ed., 1951, pp. 164–65.
44. Howe, *op. cit.*, pp. 69–109.
45. A. L. Bawley and George Henry Wood. The statistics of wages in the United Kingdom during the last hundred years. *JRSS*, 62 (1899), p. 708.

46. For this document, see note 6, above.
47. P.R.O. PROB 11/1045/357.
48. P.R.O. PROB 11/908/148.
49. John Cheney and Sons, Ltd., Banbury. Archives. Memoranda written in *The new daily journal* (1759).
50. Piper, *op. cit.*, p. 194.
51. Philip, *op. cit.*, p. 23.
52. Patricia Hernlund. William Strahan's standard charges for printing, 1738–1785. *SB*, 20 (1967), pp. 89–111.
53. Keith I. D. Maslen. Printing charges: inference and evidence. *SB*, 24 (1971), pp. 90–98.
54. Welsh, *op. cit.*, p. 358. J. Morris Jones (ed.). *The Letters of Goronwy Owen*. Liverpool, 1914, p. 21.
55. Smith, *op. cit.*, vol. 2, p. 350.
56. Patricia Hernlund. Problems of editing business and trade manuscripts. In *Eighteenth century English books. Proceedings of a conference held at San Francisco June 25–28, 1975*. Chicago (Association of College and Research Libraries), 1976, Figure 2, after p. 47.
57. A rather later example perhaps helps to illustrate this. In 1823, John Hall of Newport, Isle of Wight, charged £2.0s.0d. a sheet for 1,000 copies of John Albin's *Companion to the Isle of Wight*, about the current London rate. The agreement is Humberside R.O. SCR 443, between pp. 195 and 196.
58. Alfred Gregory. *Robert Raikes: journalist and philanthropist*. London, 1877, pp. 16–18.
59. P.R.O. PROB 11/1326/483.
60. P.R.O. PROB 11/1045/357.
61. Dickinson, *op. cit.*, pp. 164–71.
62. *The Ipswich Journal*, 24 (21–28 Jan. 1721).
63. *Records of the Borough of Nottingham*, vol. 6, p. 120.
64. John Cheney and Sons, Ltd., Banbury. Archives. Record of customers' accounts, 1794–1805.
65. He is so recorded in *The Universal British Directory*.
66. A. H. Shorter. *Paper mills and paper makers in England 1495–1800*. Hilversum, 1957, p. 225.
67. Again, so recorded in *The Universal British Directory*.
68. Alfred Beesley. *The history of Banbury*. London, 1841, pp. 534, 535.
69. Charles Hadfield. *The canals of the east midlands*. Newton Abbot, 2nd ed., 1970, p. 274.
70. Judd is in *The Universal British Directory*. See also *VCH Oxon.*, vol. 10, pp. 12, 87.
71. *Ibid.*, p. 14, for Watson's players. For Cobb and Cobb, see Audrey M. Taylor. *Gillets. Bankers at Banbury and Oxford*. Oxford, 1964, p. 5, n. 1, pp. 11–12.
72. Cranfield, *op. cit.*, pp. 48–64. Wiles, *Freshest advices*, pp. 41–92.

73. Hunt, *op. cit.*, pp. 3–4, 81, 95. Victor E. Neuburg. *Chapbooks.* London, 2nd ed., 1972, pp. 56–60. Thomson, *op. cit.*, pp. 8–9, 13, 14.
74. Hunt, *op. cit.*, p. 20. Charles Hindley. *The history of the Catnach Press.* London, 1886, pp. 1–8.
75. C. J. Hunt and Peter C. G. Isaac. *The regulation of the book trade in Newcastle-upon-Tyne at the beginning of the nineteenth century.* Newcastle-upon-Tyne (History of the Book Trade in the North), 1976, pp. 2, 12–13.
76. Neuburg, The Diceys, *passim.*
77. By Mr D. F. Foxon in his Sandars Lectures on the stamp Act of 1712, delivered at Cambridge in 1978.
78. Plomer, *op. cit.*, p. 29. 'Bence' of Wootton-under-Edge is listed by Pendred, *ed. cit.*, p. 37, which can leave no doubt that there was such a person in the village in the 1780s, and that he was a printer. The printer in the 1720s was, presumably, of an earlier generation. My only doubt about these imprints is that Bence's name might have been used by a pirate closer to the wrath of the copyright owners. For examples of the imprints, see *Catalogue of English and American chapbooks and broadside ballads in Harvard College Library.* Cambridge, Mass., 1905, nos. 59, 403, 477, 605, 1860, 2123.
79. Cheney, *op. cit.*, *passim.*
80. Trewin and King, *op. cit.*, pp. 23–24.
81. Cambridge University Library. Madden 18 (1352), (1353).
82. Feather, John Clay. For information on the trade in Warwickshire, I am indebted to Mr R. J. Chamberlaine-Brothers of Warwickshire R.O.
83. There are hundreds of them in B.L., and more in the Madden collection at Cambridge University Library.
84. Cambridge University Library. Madden 23 (681). *VCH Wilts.*, vol. 6, pp. 107, 108, 121.
85. *An excellent ballad . . . of King Richard the Third.* [c.1730?] Cambridge University Library. Madden 2 (476).
86. Wiles, *Freshest advices*, p. 428.
87. Cyprian Blagden. The English Stock of the Stationers' Company in the time of the Stuarts. *The Library*, 5th ser., 12 (1957), pp. 167–86. For almanacs, see Bernard Capp. *Astrology and the popular press. English almanacs 1500–1800.* London, 1979.
88. Plomer, *op. cit.*, p. 64. Plomer, Bushnell, and Dix, *op. cit.*, p. 43. Cyprian Blagden. Thomas Carnan and the almanac monopoly. *SB*, 14 (1961), pp. 22–43.
89. Henry Fielding. *Joseph Andrews.* Ed. Martin C. Batterstin. Oxford, 1967, p. 67.
90. Kenneth Monkman. The bibliography of the early editions of *Tristram Shandy. The Library*, 5th ser., 25 (1970), pp. 11–22. Lewis P. Curtis. The first printer of *Tristram Shandy. PMLA*, 47 (1932), 777–89.
91. Joseph Cottle. *Reminiscences of Samuel Taylor Coleridge and Robert*

Southey. London, 1847, pp. 2, 185. Robert W. Daniel. The publication of the *Lyrical Ballads*. *MLR*, 33 (1938), pp. 406–10. D. F. Foxon. The printing of *Lyrical Ballads*. *The Library*, 5th ser., 9 (1954), pp. 221–41.

92. Joyce Hemlow (ed.). *The journal and letters of Fanny Burney*, vol. I. *1791–1792*. Oxford, 1972, p. 22.

93. Bodleian Library, Oxford. MS Eng. lett. c. 355, f. 73. 'Mr Baldwin' is Robert Baldwin, a leading bookseller (Maxted, *op. cit.*, p. 11); 'the Row' is Paternoster Row, the centre of the London trade.

94. *Parliamentary history*, vol. 27, col. 1085. See above, pp. 5–10, for the context.

95. *The Gentleman's Magazine*, 75 (1809), p. 1179. *Ibid.*, 89 (1819), pp. 384–85.

96. Bodleian Library, Oxford. MS. lett. c. 357, f. 180.

97. *Ibid.*, f. 181.

98. *Ibid.*, f. 180.

99. *Ibid.*, f. 183.

100. Bodleian Library, Oxford. MS Eng. lett. c. 372, f. 124$^\mathrm{v}$.

101. *DNB* (Coles).

102. J. B. Figgis (ed.). *The Countess of Huntingdon and her connexion*. London, 1891, pp. 42–45. J. C. Ryle. *The Christian leaders of the last century*. London, 1899, pp. 149–79.

103. *DNB* (Orton).

104. Bodleian Library, Oxford. J. Pros. 322.

105. Plomer, Bushnell, and Dix, *op. cit.*, p. 87.

106. *VCH Lancs.*, vol. 3, pp. 305–08.

107. H. McLachlan. *Warrington Academy, its history and influence*. Manchester (Cheetham Society, new ser., 107), 1943.

108. A. J. Hawkes. *Lancashire printed books. A bibliography of all books printed in Lancashire down to the year 1800*. Wigan, 1925, nos. 810, 811.

109. *Ibid.*, no. 812.

110. Letters and papers of the Rev. John Seddon. No. III. *The Christian Reformer*, new ser., 10 (1854), p. 628.

111. Hawkes, *op. cit.*, nos. 810–1013. McLachlan, *Warrington*, p. 226.

112. McLachlan, *English education*, p. 225.

113. *The literary life of the late Thomas Pennant, Esq., by himself*. London, 1793, p. 36. McLachlan, *Warrington*, pp. 41, 84–85.

114. *Ibid.*, p. 84. McLachlan, *English education*, p. 119.

115. Gerald P. Tyson. *Joseph Johnson: a liberal publisher*. Iowa City, Iowa, 1979, pp. 17–21.

116. Frida Knight. *University rebel. The life of William Frend*. London, 1971, p. 99.

117. John Walsh. Methodism at the end of the eighteenth century. *In* Rupert Davies and Gordon Rupp (ed.). *A history of the Methodist Church in Great Britain*, vol. I. London, 1965, pp. 277–78.

118. John F. Fulton. The place of William Withering in scientific medicine. *JHMAS*, 8 (1953), pp. 1–15.

119. H. G. Salter (ed.). *Remarks and collections of Thomas Hearne, vol. XI (Dec. 9, 1731–June 10, 1735)*. Oxford (Oxford Historical Society, 72), 1921, p. 23. Hearne also noted the authorship on the title-page of his copy of the book, now Bodleian Library, Oxford. 8° Rawl. 661. For Wallis, see Forster, *op. cit.*, vol. 4, p. 1560 (Wallace). In Hearne's opinion, the book, 'a little thing', was 'mean' and 'rude'.
120. A. L. Owen. *Those famous Druids*. Oxford, 1962, pp. 101–37.
121. Ulrich Thieme and Felix Becker. *Allgemeines Lexicon der Bildenden Künstler*. Leipzig, 37 vols., 1907–50, vol. 14, pp. 568–69.
122. Charles Chenevix Trench. *The royal malady*. London, 1964, pp. 8–9.
123. There is no adequate bibliography of eighteenth-century local history, and it is a great desideratum. Apart from Richard Gough. *British topography*. London, 2nd ed., 2 vols., 1780, there is only the incomplete list in G. E. Fussell. *The exploration of England: a select bibliography of travel and topography: 1570–1815*. London, 1935, pp. 25–44.

Index of the Provincial Book Trade

General Index

Book titles are indexed under the heading Books, and periodical titles under the heading Periodicals. Newspaper titles will be found in the Index of the Provincial Book Trade. General discussions of the history and organisation of the trade are analytically indexed under the headings Authors, Booksellers, Bookselling, Bookshops, Newspapers, Paper trade, Printers, Printing, and Publishing. The contents of the inventories in Appendices I–III are not indexed.

173

General Index

Books – *cont.*
  Practical Discourses of God's Sovereignty 113–14, 139
  Practical Scrivener, The 36
  Prophecies of the Second Book of Esdras, The 15
  Reading Made Easy 24
  Rites and Ceremonies of the Greek Church in Russia, The 52
  Robinson Crusoe 104
  Select Hymns 16
  Short and Plain Exposition of the Old Testament, A 114–15, 139
  Sketch of the Ancient and Present State of Sherwood Forest, A 119
  State of the Prisons in England and Wales, The 117
  Statutes at Large, The 75
  Survey of the City of Worcester, A 120
  Thoughts on the Effects of the Application and Abstraction of Stimuli on the Human Body 66
  Thurloe State Papers 52–53
  Tour of Scotland 116
  Treatise of English Particles 79
  Trials for Adultery 50
  Tristram Shandy 110
  Two Discourses or Demonstrations on Religion and Virtue 78
  Vicar of Wakefield 4, 104
  Vindication of the Divinity of Jesus Christ 110
  Voyage to Abbysinia 94
  Voyage to the West Coast of Africa, A 78
  Wright's Antiquities of Rutland with Additions 112
  Writer's Time Redeemed, The 113, 138
Booksellers (*see also under individual booksellers in Index of the Provincial Book Trade*)
  London: catalogues 45–47; distributors of provincial books 111–14
  provincial: bankruptcies 30, 93–96; catalogues 90–91; charitable donations 92–93; distributors of London books 61–62, 64–67; family background of apprentices 89–90; family connections between firms 88; newsagents 17–19, 21, 23–25, 65, 67; numbers 28–29; political activities 92; property owners 91; relations with London booksellers 4–10, 64–67; religious affiliations 93; social status 91–93; subscription agents 52–53; wealth 90–93
Bookselling (*see also under individual booksellers in Index of the Provincial Book Trade*)
  advertising 44–53
  apprenticeship 89–90
  combined with other occupations: grocers 85; insurance agents 84–85; medicine vendors 83–84; newsagents 17–19, 21, 23–25, 65, 67; schoolmasters 35; Stamp Distributors 85–87; stationers 80–82
  development of shopkeeping 12–15
  discounts 55–59
  itinerant 12–13
  Lackington's opinions 69
  market for books 33–43
  prices of books 57
  second-hand trade 79
  trade terms 55–59
Bookshops
  fittings 72–74
  premises 70–74
  stock 73–80
Bowden, George 39
British Fire Office 85
Bunyan, John 6, 40
Burdon, William 7
Burkitt, William 38
Burlington, Charles 49
Burnet, Gilbert 38

Caldecott, Thomas 36
Campbell, R. 69
Carter, Mr, of Banbury 106

Carter, Edmund 120
Catalogues
  Annual Catalogue 46
  British National Bibliography 46
  Catalogue of the Most Vendible Books in England 45
  Complete Catalogue of Modern Books 46
  English Catalogue, The 46
  London Catalogue, The 46
  Mercurius Librarius 45
  Monthly Catalogue, The 45–46
  Term Catalogues 45–46, 59
Cave, Edward 19–21, 46–47, 94
Champion, Joseph 36
Chapbook trade 107–08
Chapbooks 40–41, 107–08
Chapmen 108
Cheap Repository Tracts 41
Circulating libraries 41–42
Clarendon, Edward Hyde, 1st Earl of 47
Classical texts 1, 34, 35, 74
Claude, Jean 48
Coleridge, Samuel Taylor 110
Coles, Elisha 114–15, 139
Congers 2–3
Copyright 2–11
Copyright Act (1710) 2, 6–7, 9
Corderius 40
Coward, Henry 111
Cowley, Charlotte 49–50

Darney, William 79
Daventry Academy 34–35
DeChare, Mr, of Horley 106
Deddington paper mill 105
Dr James's Fever Powder 84
Dodson, James 36
Dyche, Thomas 33–34

Education 33–35
Ely Pamphlet Club 42
Enfield, John 116, 117
Eton College 35

Fawcett, John 49
Floyer, Sir John 15
Foot, William 39–40
Foxe, John 38
Frend, William 117

Gentleman, Robert 114
Golby, James 106
Goldsmith, Oliver 4, 104
Grammar schools 35
Green, Valentine 119–20
Griffiths, Ralph 50
Grocery trade 85
Guide books 110–11

Harris, Mr, of Bicester 106
Harrod, William *see* Index of the Provincial Book Trade
Hasted, Edward 120
Hawtyn, Joseph 105
Hearne, Thomas 166 (n. 119)
Hervey, Thomas 113, 138
Hitchcock, James 54
Howard, John 117
Hoyle, Edward 79
Hunt, Mr, of Aynho 106
Huntingdon, Anne, Countess of 113
Hurd, Richard 78
Hutchinson, William 118

Import of Books Act (1739) 7–8
Imprints, interpretation of 59–62, 110–11
Insurance 84–85

General Index